The Books of

KAHLIL GIBRAN

"His power came from some great reservoir of spiritual life else it could not have been so universal and so potent, but the majesty and beauty of the language with which he clothed it were all his own." — CLAUDE BRAGDON

PUBLISHED BY ALFRED A. KNOPF

THE GARDEN

of

THE PROPHET

THE GARDEN
of
THE PROPHET

BY

KAHLIL GIBRAN

1968

NEW YORK : ALFRED·A·KNOPF

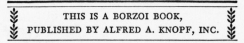

THIS IS A BORZOI BOOK,
PUBLISHED BY ALFRED A. KNOPF, INC.

Twenty Third Printing

THE GARDEN
of
THE PROPHET

ALMUSTAFA, the chosen and the beloved, who was a noon unto his own day, returned to the isle of his birth in the month of Tichreen, which is the month of remembrance.

And as his ship approached the harbour, he stood upon its prow, and his mariners were about him. And there was a homecoming in his heart.

And he spoke, and the sea was in his voice, and he said: "Behold, the isle of our birth. Even here the earth heaved us, a song and a riddle; a song unto the sky, a riddle unto the earth; and what is there between earth and sky that shall carry the song and solve the riddle save our own passion?

"The sea yields us once more to these shores. We are but another wave of her waves. She sends us forth to sound her speech, but how shall we do so unless we break the symmetry of our heart on rock and sand?

3

"For this is the law of mariners and the sea: If you would freedom, you must needs turn to mist. The formless is for ever seeking form, even as the countless nebulæ would become suns and moons; and we who have sought much and return now to this isle, rigid moulds, we must become mist once more and learn of the beginning. And what is there that shall live and rise unto the heights except it be broken unto passion and freedom?

"For ever shall we be in quest of the shores, that we may sing and be heard. But what of the wave that breaks where no ear shall hear? It is the unheard in us that nurses our deeper sorrow. Yet it is also the unheard which carves our soul to form and fashions our destiny."

Then one of his mariners came forth and said: "Master, you have captained our longing for this harbour, and behold, we have come. Yet you speak of sorrow, and of hearts that shall be broken."

And he answered him and said: "Did I

not speak of freedom, and of the mist which is our greater freedom? Yet it is in pain I make pilgrimage to the isle where I was born, even like unto a ghost of one slain come to kneel before those who have slain him."

And another mariner spoke and said: "Behold, the multitudes on the sea-wall. In their silence they have foretold even the day and the hour of your coming, and they have gathered from their fields and vineyards in their loving need, to await you."

And Almustafa looked afar upon the multitudes, and his heart was mindful of their yearning, and he was silent.

Then a cry came from the people, and it was a cry of remembrance and of entreaty.

And he looked upon his mariners and said: "And what have I brought them? A hunter was I, in a distant land. With aim and might I have spent the golden arrows they gave me, but I have brought down no game. I followed not the arrows. Mayhap they are spreading now in the sun with the pinions of wounded eagles that would not fall to earth. And mayhap the arrow-heads have fallen into the hands of those who had need of them for bread and wine.

"I know not where they have spent their flight, but this I know: they have made their curve in the sky.

"Even so, love's hand is still upon me, and you, my mariners, still sail my vision, and I shall not be dumb. I shall cry out when the hand of the seasons is upon my throat, and I shall sing my words when my lips are burned with flames."

And they were troubled in their hearts because he spoke these things. And one said: "Master, teach us all, and mayhap because your blood flows in our veins, and our breath is of your fragrance, we shall understand."

Then he answered them, and the wind was in his voice, and he said: "Brought you me to the isle of my birth to be a teacher? Not yet have I been caged by wisdom. Too young am I and too verdant to speak of

6

aught but self, which is for ever the deep calling upon the deep.

"Let him who would have wisdom seek it in the buttercup or in a pinch of red clay. I am still the singer. Still I shall sing the earth, and I shall sing your lost dreaming that walks the day between sleep and sleep. But I shall gaze upon the sea."

And now the ship entered the harbour and reached the sea-wall, and he came thus to the isle of his birth and stood once more amongst his own people. And a great cry arose from their hearts so that the loneliness of his home-coming was shaken within him.

And they were silent awaiting his word, but he answered them not, for the sadness of memory was upon him, and he said in his heart: "Have I said that I shall sing? Nay, I can but open my lips that the voice of life may come forth and go out to the wind for joy and support."

Then Karima, she who had played with him, a child, in the Garden of his mother, spoke and said: "Twelve years have you hidden your face from us, and for twelve years have we hungered and thirsted for your voice."

And he looked upon her with exceeding tenderness, for it was she who had closed the eyes of his mother when the white wings of death had gathered her.

And he answered and said: "Twelve years? Said you twelve years, Karima? I measured not my longing with the starry rod, nor did I sound the depth thereof. For love when love is homesick exhausts time's measurements and time's soundings.

"There are moments that hold æons of separation. Yet parting is naught but an exhaustion of the mind. Perhaps we have not parted."

And Almustafa looked upon the people, and he saw them all, the youth and the aged, the stalwart and the puny, those who were ruddy with the touch of wind and sun, and those also who were of pallid countenance; and upon their face a light of longing and of questioning.

8

And one spoke and said: "Master, life has dealt bitterly with our hopes and our desires. Our hearts are troubled, and we do not understand. I pray you, comfort us, and open to us the meanings of our sorrows."

And his heart was moved with compassion, and he said: "Life is older than all things living; even as beauty was wingèd ere the beautiful was born on earth, and even as truth was truth ere it was uttered.

"Life sings in our silences, and dreams in our slumber. Even when we are beaten and low, Life is enthroned and high. And when we weep, Life smiles upon the day, and is free even when we drag our chains.

"Oftentimes we call Life bitter names, but only when we ourselves are bitter and dark. And we deem her empty and unprofitable, but only when the soul goes wandering in desolate places, and the heart is drunken with overmindfulness of self.

"Life is deep and high and distant; and though only your vast vision can reach

9

even her feet, yet she is near; and though only the breath of your breath reaches her heart, the shadow of your shadow crosses her face, and the echo of your faintest cry becomes a spring and an autumn in her breast.

"And Life is veiled and hidden, even as your greater self is hidden and veiled. Yet when Life speaks, all the winds become words; and when she speaks again, the smiles upon your lips and the tears in your eyes turn also into words. When she sings, the deaf hear and are held; and when she comes walking, the sightless behold her and are amazed and follow her in wonder and astonishment."

And he ceased from speaking, and a vast silence enfolded the people, and in the silence there was an unheard song, and they were comforted of their loneliness and their aching.

And he left them straightway and fol-
lowed the path which led to his Garden,
which was the Garden of his mother and his
father, wherein they lay asleep, they and
their forefathers.

And there were those who would have
followed after him, seeing that it was a
home-coming, and he was alone, for there
was not one left of all his kin to spread the
feast of welcome, after the manner of his
people.

But the captain of his ship counselled
them saying: "Suffer him to go upon his
way. For his bread is the bread of alone-
ness, and in his cup is the wine of remem-
brance, which he would drink alone."

And his mariners held their steps, for
they knew it was even as the captain of the
ship had told them. And all those who
gathered upon the sea-wall restrained the
feet of their desire.

Only Karima went after him, a little way, yearning over his aloneness and his memories. And she spoke not, but turned and went unto her own house, and in the garden under the almond-tree she wept, yet knew not wherefore.

And Almustafa came and found the Garden of his mother and his father, and he entered in, and closed the gate that no man might come after him.

And for forty days and forty nights he dwelt alone in that house and that Garden, and none came, not even unto the gate, for it was closed, and all the people knew that he would be alone.

And when the forty days and nights were ended, Almustafa opened the gate that they might come in.

And there came nine men to be with him in the Garden; three mariners from his own ship; three who had served in the Temple; and three who had been his comrades in play when they were but children together. And these were his disciples.

And on a morning his disciples sat around him, and there were distances and remembrances in his eyes. And that disciple

13

who was called Hafiz said unto him: "Master, tell us of the city of Orphalese, and of that land wherein you tarried those twelve years."

And Almustafa was silent, and he looked away toward the hills and toward the vast ether, and there was a battle in his silence.

Then he said: "My friends and my road-fellows, pity the nation that is full of beliefs and empty of religion.

"Pity the nation that wears a cloth it does not weave, eats a bread it does not harvest, and drinks a wine that flows not from its own winepress.

"Pity the nation that acclaims the bully as hero, and that deems the glittering conqueror bountiful.

"Pity a nation that despises a passion in its dream, yet submits in its awakening.

"Pity the nation that raises not its voice save when it walks in a funeral, boasts not except among its ruins, and will rebel not save when its neck is laid between the sword and the block.

"Pity the nation whose statesman is a fox, whose philosopher is a juggler, and whose art is the art of patching and mimicking.

"Pity the nation that welcomes its new ruler with trumpetings, and farewells him with hootings, only to welcome another with trumpetings again.

"Pity the nation whose sages are dumb with years and whose strong men are yet in the cradle.

"Pity the nation divided into fragments, each fragment deeming itself a nation."

And one said: "Speak to us of that which is moving in your own heart even now."

And he looked upon that one, and there was in his voice a sound like a star singing, and he said: "In your waking dream, when you are hushed and listening to your deeper self, your thoughts, like snow-flakes, fall and flutter and garment all the sounds of your spaces with white silence.

"And what are waking dreams but clouds that bud and blossom on the sky-tree of your heart? And what are your thoughts but the petals which the winds of your heart scatter upon the hills and its fields?

"And even as you wait for peace until the formless within you takes form, so shall the cloud gather and drift until the Blessed Fingers shape its grey desire to little crystal suns and moons and stars."

Then Sarkis, he who was the half-doubter, spoke and said: "But spring shall come, and all the snows of our dreams and our thoughts shall melt and be no more."

And he answered saying: "When Spring comes to seek His beloved among the slumbering groves and vineyards, the snows shall indeed melt and shall run in streams to seek the river in the valley, to be the cup-bearer to the myrtle-trees and laurel.

"So shall the snow of your heart melt when your Spring is come, and thus shall your secret run in streams to seek the river of life in the valley. And the river shall enfold your secret and carry it to the great sea.

"All things shall melt and turn into songs when Spring comes. Even the stars, the vast snow-flakes that fall slowly upon the larger fields, shall melt into singing streams. When the sun of His face shall arise above the wider horizon, then what frozen symmetry would not turn into liquid melody? And who among you would not be the cup-bearer to the myrtle and the laurel?

"It was but yesterday that you were

moving with the moving sea, and you were shoreless and without a self. Then the wind, the breath of Life, wove you, a veil of light on her face; then her hand gathered you and gave you form, and with a head held high you sought the heights. But the sea followed after you, and her song is still with you. And though you have forgotten your parentage, she will for ever assert her motherhood, and for ever will she call you unto her.

"In your wanderings among the mountains and the desert you will always remember the depth of her cool heart. And though oftentimes you will not know for what you long, it is indeed for her vast and rhythmic peace.

"And how else can it be? In grove and in bower when the rain dances in leaves upon the hill, when snow falls, a blessing and a covenant; in the valley when you lead your flocks to the river; in your fields where brooks, like silver streams, join together the green garment; in your gardens when the early dews mirror the heavens;

18

in your meadows when the mist of evening half veils your way; in all these the sea is with you, a witness to your heritage, and a claim upon your love.

"It is the snow-flake in you running down to the sea."

And on a morning as they walked in the Garden, there appeared before the gate a woman, and it was Karima, she whom Almustafa had loved even as a sister in his boyhood. And she stood without, asking nothing, nor knocking with her hand upon the gate, but only gazing with longing and sadness into the Garden.

And Almustafa saw the desire upon her eyelids, and with swift steps he came to the wall and the gate and opened unto her, and she came in and was made welcome.

And she spoke and said: "Wherefore have you withdrawn yourself from us altogether, that we may not live in the light of your countenance? For behold, these many years have we loved you and waited with longing for your safe return. And now the people cry for you and would have speech with you; and I am their messenger come to beseech you that you will show yourself to the people, and speak to them out of your wisdom, and comfort the broken of heart and instruct our foolishness."

And looking upon her, he said: "Call me not wise unless you call all men wise. A young fruit am I, still clinging to the branch, and it was only yesterday that I was but a blossom.

"And call none among you foolish, for in truth we are neither wise nor foolish. We are green leaves upon the tree of life, and life itself is beyond wisdom, and surely beyond foolishness.

"And have I indeed withdrawn myself from you? Know you not that there is no distance save that which the soul does not span in fancy? And when the soul shall span that distance, it becomes a rhythm in the soul.

"The space that lies between you and your near neighbour unbefriended is indeed greater than that which lies between you and your beloved who dwells beyond seven lands and seven seas.

"For in remembrance there are no distances; and only in oblivion is there a gulf that neither your voice nor your eye can abridge.

"Between the shores of the oceans and the summit of the highest mountain there is a secret road which you must needs travel ere you become one with the sons of earth.

"And between your knowledge and your understanding there is a secret path which you must needs discover ere you become one with man, and therefore one with yourself.

"Between your right hand that gives and your left hand that receives there is a great space. Only by deeming them both giving and receiving can you bring them into spacelessness, for it is only in knowing that you have naught to give and naught to receive that you can overcome space.

"Verily the vastest distance is that which lies between your sleep-vision and your wakefulness; and between that which is but a deed and that which is a desire.

"And there is still another road which

you must needs travel ere you become one with Life. But of that road I shall not speak now, seeing that you are weary already of travelling."

Then he went forth with the woman, he and the nine, even unto the market-place, and he spoke to the people, his friends and his neighbours, and there was joy in their hearts and upon their eyelids.

And he said: "You grow in sleep, and live your fuller life in your dreaming. For all your days are spent in thanksgiving for that which you have received in the stillness of the night.

"Oftentimes you think and speak of night as the season of rest, yet in truth night is the season of seeking and finding.

"The day gives unto you the power of knowledge and teaches your fingers to become versed in the art of receiving; but it is night that leads you to the treasure-house of Life.

"The sun teaches to all things that grow their longing for the light. But it is night that raises them to the stars.

24

"It is indeed the stillness of the night that weaves a wedding-veil over the trees in the forest, and the flowers in the garden, and then spreads the lavish feast and makes ready the nuptial chamber; and in that holy silence tomorrow is conceived in the womb of Time.

"Thus it is with you, and thus, in seeking, you find meat and fulfilment. And though at dawn your awakening erases the memory, the board of dreams is for ever spread, and the nuptial chamber waiting."

And he was silent for a space, and they also, awaiting his word. Then he spoke again, saying: "You are spirits though you move in bodies; and, like oil that burns in the dark, you are flames though held in lamps.

"If you were naught save bodies, then my standing before you and speaking unto you would be but emptiness, even as the dead calling unto the dead. But this is not so. All that is deathless in you is free unto the day and the night and cannot be housed

25

nor fettered, for this is the will of the Most High. You are His breath even as the wind that shall be neither caught nor caged. And I also am the breath of His breath."

And he went from their midst walking swiftly and entered again into the Garden.

And Sarkis, he who was the half-doubter, spoke and said: "And what of ugliness, Master? You speak never of ugliness."

And Almustafa answered him, and there was a whip in his words, and he said: "My friend, what man shall call you inhospitable if he shall pass by your house, yet would not knock at your door?

"And who shall deem you deaf and unmindful if he shall speak to you in a strange tongue of which you understand nothing?

"Is it not that which you have never striven to reach, into whose heart you have never desired to enter, that you deem ugliness?

"If ugliness is aught, indeed, it is but the

26

scales upon our eyes, and the wax filling our ears.

"Call nothing ugly, my friend, save the fear of a soul in the presence of its own memories."

And upon a day as they sat in the long shadows of the white poplars, one spoke saying: "Master, I am afraid of time. It passes over us and robs us of our youth, and what does it give in return?"

And he answered and said: "Take up now a handful of good earth. Do you find in it a seed, and perhaps a worm? If your hand were spacious and enduring enough, the seed might become a forest, and the worm a flock of angels. And forget not that the years which turn seeds to forests, and worms to angels, belong to this *Now*, all of the years, this very *Now*.

"And what are the seasons of the years save your own thoughts changing? Spring is an awakening in your breast, and summer but a recognition of your own fruitfulness. Is not autumn the ancient in you singing a lullaby to that which is still a child in your being? And what, I ask you, is winter

28

save sleep big with the dreams of all the other seasons."

And then Mannus, the inquisitive disciple, looked about him and he saw plants in flower cleaving unto the sycamore-tree. And he said: "Behold the parasites, Master. What say you of them? They are thieves with weary eyelids who steal the light from the steadfast children of the sun, and make fair of the sap that runneth into their branches and their leaves."

And he answered him saying: "My friend, we are all parasites. We who labour to turn the sod into pulsing life are not above those who receive life directly from the sod without knowing the sod.

"Shall a mother say to her child: 'I give you back to the forest, which is your greater mother, for you weary me, heart and hand'?

"Or shall the singer rebuke his own song, saying: 'Return now to the cave of echoes from whence you came, for your voice consumes my breath'?

"And shall the shepherd say to his yearling: 'I have no pasture whereunto I may lead you; therefore be cut off and become a sacrifice for this cause'?

"Nay, my friend, all these things are answered even before they are asked, and, like your dreams, are fulfilled ere you sleep.

"We live upon one another according to the law, ancient and timeless. Let us live thus in loving-kindness. We seek one another in our aloneness, and we walk the road when we have no hearth to sit beside.

"My friends and my brothers, the wider road is your fellow-man.

"These plants that live upon the tree draw the milk of the earth in the sweet stillness of night, and the earth in her tranquil dreaming sucks at the breast of the sun.

"And the sun, even as you and I and all there is, sits in equal honour at the banquet of the Prince whose door is always open and whose board is always spread.

"Mannus, my friend, all there is lives

always upon all there is; and all there is lives in the faith, shoreless, upon the bounty of the Most High."

And on a morning when the sky was yet pale with dawn, they walked all together in the Garden and looked unto the East and were silent in the presence of the rising sun.

And after a while Almustafa pointed with his hand, and he said: "The image of the morning sun in a dewdrop is not less than the sun. The reflection of life in your soul is not less than life.

"The dewdrop mirrors the light because it is one with light, and you reflect life because you and life are one.

"When darkness is upon you, say: 'This darkness is dawn not yet born; and though night's travail be full upon me, yet shall dawn be born unto me even as unto the hills.'

"The dewdrop rounding its sphere in the dusk of the lily is not unlike yourself gathering your soul in the heart of God.

32

... أيّها... نقطة الندى تكبر... أكبر... إلخ من... قطرة الندى

Dew-drops

The image of the morning sun in
a dew drop is not less than the
sun

The reflection of life in your
soul is not less than life.

A dew drop mirrors the
light because it is one with
light,

And you reflect life because
you and life are one.

When darkness is upon
you say," This darkness is
dawn not yet born

" And though night's
child bearing is upon me and
night's child birth shall be
upon me,

" Yet shall dawn be born

unto me,

Even as unto the hills and the valleys"

A dew drop rounding its sphere in the dusk of the lily is not unlike yourself gathering your soul in the heart of God.

Shall a dew drop say:
"But once in a thousand years am even a dew drop?"
And knows not that all light (of all the years) is shining in its circle.

— o —

"Shall a dewdrop say: 'But once in a thousand years am I even a dewdrop,' speak you and answer it saying: 'Know you not that the light of all the years is shining in your circle?' "

And on an evening a great storm visited the place, and Almustafa and his disciples, the nine, went within and sat about the fire and were still and silent.

Then one of the disciples said: "I am alone, Master, and the hoofs of the hours beat heavily upon my breast."

And Almustafa rose up and stood in their midst, and he said in a voice like unto the sound of a great wind: "Alone! And what of it? You came alone, and alone shall you pass into the mist.

"Therefore drink your cup alone and in silence. The autumn days have given other lips other cups and filled them with wine bitter and sweet, even as they have filled your cup.

"Drink your cup alone though it taste of your own blood and tears, and praise life for the gift of thirst. For without thirst your heart is but the shore of a barren sea, songless and without a tide.

"Drink your cup alone, and drink it with cheers.

"Raise it high above your head and drink deep to those who drink alone.

"Once I sought the company of men and sat with them at their banquet-tables and drank deep with them; but their wine did not rise to my head, nor did it flow into my bosom. It only descended to my feet. My wisdom was left dry and my heart was locked and sealed. Only my feet were with them in their fog.

"And I sought the company of men no more, nor drank wine with them at their board.

"Therefore I say unto you, though the hoofs of the hours beat heavily upon your bosom, what of it? It is well for you to drink your cup of sorrow alone, and your cup of joy shall you drink alone also."

And on a day, as Phardrous, the Greek, walked in the Garden, he struck his foot upon a stone and he was angered. And he turned and picked up the stone, saying in a low voice: "O dead thing in my path!" and he flung away the stone.

And Almustafa, the chosen and the beloved, said: "Why say you: 'O dead thing'? Have you been thus long in this Garden and know not that there is nothing dead here? All things live and glow in the knowledge of the day and the majesty of the night. You and the stone are one. There is a difference only in heart-beats. Your heart beats a little faster, does it, my friend? Ay, but it is not so tranquil.

"Its rhythm may be another rhythm, but I say unto you that if you sound the depths of your soul and scale the heights of space, you shall hear but one melody, and in that melody the stone and the star sing, the one

36

with the other, in perfect unison.

"If my words reach not your under-standing, then let be until another dawn. If you have cursed this stone because in your blindness you have stumbled upon it, then would you curse a star if so be your head should encounter it in the sky. But the day will come when you will gather stones and stars as a child plucks the valley-lilies, and then shall you know that all these things are living and fragrant."

And on the first day of the week when the sounds of the temple bells sought their ears, one spoke and said: "Master, we hear much talk of God hereabout. What say you of God, and who is He in very truth?"

And he stood before them like a young tree, fearless of wind or tempest, and he answered saying: "Think now, my comrades and beloved, of a heart that contains all your hearts, a love that encompasses all your loves, a spirit that envelops all your spirits, a voice enfolding all your voices, and a silence deeper than all your silences, and timeless.

"Seek now to perceive in your selfulness a beauty more enchanting than all things beautiful, a song more vast than the songs of the sea and the forest, a majesty seated upon a throne for which Orion is but a footstool, holding a sceptre in which the

Pleiades are naught save the glimmer of dewdrops.

"You have sought always only food and shelter, a garment and a staff; seek now One who is neither an aim for your arrows nor a stony cave to shield you from the elements.

"And if my words are a rock and a riddle, then seek, none the less, that your hearts may be broken, and that your questionings may bring you unto the love and the wisdom of the Most High, whom men call God."

And they were silent, every one, and they were perplexed in their heart; and Almustafa was moved with compassion for them, and he gazed with tenderness upon them and said: "Let us speak no more now of God the Father. Let us speak rather of the gods, your neighbours, and of your brothers, the elements that move about your houses and your fields.

"You would rise in fancy unto the cloud, and you deem it height; and you would pass over the vast sea and claim it to be distance. But I say unto you that when you sow a seed in the earth, you reach a greater height; and when you hail the beauty of the morning to your neighbour, you cross a greater sea.

"Too often do you sing God, the Infinite, and yet in truth you hear not the song. Would that you might listen to the songbirds, and to the leaves that forsake the branch when the wind passes by, and forget not, my friends, that these sing only when they are separated from the branch!

"Again I bid you to speak not so freely of God, who is your All, but speak rather and understand one another, neighbour unto neighbour, a god unto a god.

"For what shall feed the fledgling in the nest if the mother bird flies skyward? And what anemone in the field shall be fulfilled unless it be husbanded by a bee from another anemone?

"It is only when you are lost in your smaller selves that you seek the sky which you call God. Would that you might find paths into your vast selves; would that you

might be less idle and pave the roads!

"My mariners and my friends, it were wiser to speak less of God, whom we cannot understand, and more of each other, whom we may understand. Yet I would have you know that we are the breath and the fragrance of God. We are God, in leaf, in flower, and oftentimes in fruit."

And on a morning when the sun was high, one of the disciples, one of those three who had played with him in childhood, approached him saying: "Master, my garment is worn, and I have no other. Give me leave to go unto the market-place and bargain that perchance I may procure me new raiment."

And Almustafa looked upon the young man, and he said: "Give me your garment." And he did so and stood naked in the noonday.

And Almustafa said in a voice that was like a young steed running upon a road: "Only the naked live in the sun. Only the artless ride the wind. And he alone who loses his way a thousand times shall have a home-coming.

"The angels are tired of the clever. And it was but yesterday that an angel said to me: 'We created hell for those who glitter.

What else but fire can erase a shining surface and melt a thing to its core?'

"And I said: 'But in creating hell you created devils to govern hell.' But the angel answered: 'Nay, hell is governed by those who do not yield to fire.'

"Wise angel! He knows the ways of men and the ways of half-men. He is one of the seraphim who come to minister unto the prophets when they are tempted by the clever. And no doubt he smiles when the prophets smile, and weeps also when they weep.

"My friends and my mariners, only the naked live in the sun. Only the rudderless can sail the greater sea. Only he who is dark with the night shall wake with the dawn, and only he who sleeps with the roots under the snow shall reach the spring.

"For you are even like roots, and like roots are you simple, yet you have wisdom from the earth. And you are silent, yet you have within your unborn branches the choir of the four winds.

"You are frail and you are formless, yet

43

you are the beginning of giant oaks, and of the half-pencilled pattern of the willows against the sky.

"Once more I say, you are but roots betwixt the dark sod and the moving heavens. And oftentimes have I seen you rising to dance with the light, but I have also seen you shy. All roots are shy. They have hidden their hearts so long that they know not what to do with their hearts.

"But May shall come, and May is a restless virgin, and she shall mother the hills and plains."

And one who had served in the Temple besought him saying: "Teach us, Master, that our words may be even as your words, a chant and an incense unto the people."

And Almustafa answered and said: "You shall rise beyond your words, but your path shall remain, a rhythm and a fragrance; a rhythm for lovers and for all who are beloved, and a fragrance for those who would live life in a garden.

"But you shall rise beyond your words to a summit whereon the star-dust falls, and you shall open your hands until they are filled; then you shall lie down and sleep like a white fledgling in a white nest, and you shall dream of your tomorrow as white violets dream of spring.

"Ay, and you shall go down deeper than your words. You shall seek the lost fountain-heads of the streams, and you shall be a hidden cave echoing the faint

45

voices of the depths which now you do not even hear.

"You shall go down deeper than your words, ay, deeper than all sounds, to the very heart of the earth, and there you shall be alone with Him who walks also upon the Milky Way."

And after a space one of the disciples asked him saying: "Master, speak to us of *being*. What is it to *be*?"

And Almustafa looked long upon him and loved him. And he stood up and walked a distance away from them; then returning, he said: "In this Garden my father and my mother lie, buried by the hands of the living; and in this Garden lie buried the seeds of yesteryear, brought hither upon the wings of the wind. A thousand times shall my mother and my father be buried here, and a thousand times shall the wind bury the seed; and a thousand years hence shall you and I and these flowers come together in this Garden even as now, and we shall *be*, loving life, and we shall *be*, dreaming of space, and we shall *be*, rising toward the sun.

"But now today to *be* is to be wise, though not a stranger to the foolish; it is to be strong, but not to the undoing of the weak; to play with young children, not as fathers, but rather as playmates who would learn their games;

"To be simple and guileless with old men and women, and to sit with them in the shade of the ancient oak-trees, though you are still walking with Spring;

"To seek a poet though he may live beyond the seven rivers, and to be at peace in his presence, nothing wanting, nothing doubting, and with no question upon your lips;

"To know that the saint and the sinner are twin brothers, whose father is our Gracious King, and that one was born but the moment before the other, wherefore we regard him as the Crowned Prince;

"To follow Beauty even when she shall lead you to the verge of the precipice; and though she is wingèd and you are wingless, and though she shall pass beyond the

47

verge, follow her, for where Beauty is not, there is nothing;

"To be a garden without walls, a vineyard without a guardian, a treasure-house for ever open to passers-by;

"To be robbed, cheated, deceived, ay, misled and trapped and then mocked, yet with it all to look down from the height of your larger self and smile, knowing that there is a spring that will come to your garden to dance in your leaves, and an autumn to ripen your grapes; knowing that if but one of your windows is open to the East, you shall never be empty; knowing that all those deemed wrongdoers and robbers, cheaters and deceivers are your brothers in need, and that you are perchance all of these in the eyes of the blessed inhabitants of that City Invisible, above this city.

"And now, to you also whose hands fashion and find all things that are needful for the comfort of our days and our nights—

"To *be* is to be a weaver with seeing fingers, a builder mindful of light and space; to be a ploughman and feel that you are hiding a treasure with every seed you sow; to be a fisherman and a hunter with a pity for the fish and for the beast, yet a still greater pity for the hunger and need of man.

"And, above all, I say this: I would have you each and every one partners to the purpose of every man, for only so shall you hope to obtain your own good purpose.

"My comrades and my beloved, be bold and not meek; be spacious and not confined; and until my final hour and yours be indeed your greater self."

And he ceased from speaking and there fell a deep gloom upon the nine, and their heart was turned away from him, for they understood not his words.

And behold, the three men who were mariners longed for the sea; and they who had served in the Temple yearned for the consolation of her sanctuary; and they who had been his playfellows desired the market-place. They all were deaf to his words, so that the sound of them returned unto him like weary and homeless birds seeking refuge.

And Almustafa walked a distance from them in the Garden, saying nothing, nor looking upon them.

And they began to reason among themselves and to seek excuse for their longing to be gone.

And behold, they turned and went every man to his own place, so that Almustafa, the chosen and the beloved, was left alone.

And when the night was fully come, he took his steps to the grave-side of his mother and sat beneath the cedar-tree which grew above the place. And there came the shadow of a great light upon the sky, and the Garden shone like a fair jewel upon the breast of earth.

And Almustafa cried out in the aloneness of his spirit, and he said:

"Heavy-laden is my soul with her own ripe fruit. Who is there would come and take and be satisfied? Is there not one who has fasted and who is kindly and generous in heart, to come and break his fast upon my first yieldings to the sun and thus ease me of the weight of mine own abundance?

"My soul is running over with the wine of the ages. Is there no thirsty one to come and drink?

"Behold, there was a man standing at the cross-roads with hands stretched forth unto the passers-by, and his hands were filled with jewels. And he called upon the passers-by, saying: 'Pity me, and take from me. In God's name, take out of my hands and console me.'

"But the passers-by only looked upon him, and none took out of his hand.

"Would rather that he were a beggar stretching forth his hand to receive—ay, a shivering hand, and brought back empty to his bosom—than to stretch it forth full of rich gifts and find none to receive.

"And behold, there was also the gracious prince who raised up his silken tents between the mountain and the desert and bade his servants to burn fire, a sign to the stranger and the wanderer; and who sent forth his slaves to watch the road that they might fetch a guest. But the roads and the paths of the desert were unyielding, and they found no one.

"Would rather that prince were a man of nowhere and nowhen, seeking food and shelter. Would that he were the wanderer with naught but his staff and an earthen

vessel. For then at nightfall would he meet with his kind, and with the poets of nowhere and nowhen, and share their beggary and their remembrances and their dreaming.

"And behold, the daughter of the great king rose from sleep and put upon her her silken raiment and her pearls and rubies, and she scattered musk upon her hair and dipped her fingers in amber. Then she descended from her tower to her garden, where the dew of night found her golden sandals.

"In the stillness of the night the daughter of the great king sought love in the garden, but in all the vast kingdom of her father there was none who was her lover.

"Would rather that she were the daughter of a ploughman, tending his sheep in a field, and returning to her father's house at eventide with the dust of the curving roads upon her feet, and the fragrance of the vineyards in the folds of her garment. And when the night is come, and the angel of the night is upon the world, she would steal her steps to the river-valley where her lover waits.

"Would that she were a nun in a cloister burning her heart for incense, that her heart may rise to the wind, and exhausting her spirit, a candle, for a light arising toward the greater light, together with all those who worship and those who love and are beloved.

"Would rather that she were a woman ancient of years, sitting in the sun and re-membering who had shared her youth."

And the night waxed deep, and Almus-tafa was dark with the night, and his spirit was as a cloud unspent. And he cried again:

"Heavy-laden is my soul with her own
    ripe fruit;
Heavy-laden is my soul with her fruit.
Who now will come and eat and be ful-
    filled?
My soul is overflowing with her wine.
Who now will pour and drink and be
    cooled of the desert heat?

"Would that I were a tree flowerless and
      fruitless,
For the pain of abundance is more bitter
      than barrenness,
And the sorrow of the rich from whom no
      one will take
Is greater than the grief of the beggar
      to whom none would give.

"Would that I were a well, dry and
      parched, and men throwing stones
      into me;
For this were better and easier to be
      borne than to be a source of living
      water
When men pass by and will not drink.

"Would that I were a reed trodden under
      foot,
For that were better than to be a lyre of
      silvery strings
In a house whose lord has no fingers
And whose children are deaf."

Now, for seven days and seven nights no man came nigh the Garden, and he was alone with his memories and his pain; for even those who had heard his words with love and patience had turned away to the pursuits of other days.

Only Karima came, with silence upon her face like a veil; and with cup and plate within her hand, drink and meat for his aloneness and his hunger. And after setting these before him, she walked her way.

And Almustafa came again to the company of the white poplars within the gate, and he sat looking upon the road. And after a while he beheld as it were a cloud of dust blown above the road and coming toward him. And from out the cloud came the nine, and before them Karima guiding them.

And Almustafa advanced and met them upon the road, and they passed through the

56

gate, and all was well, as though they had gone their path but an hour ago.

They came in and supped with him at his frugal board, after that Karima had laid upon it the bread and the fish and poured the last of the wine into the cups. And as she poured, she besought the Master saying: "Give me leave that I go into the city and fetch wine to replenish your cups, for this is spent."

And he looked upon her, and in his eyes were a journey and a far country, and he said: "Nay, for it is sufficient unto the hour."

And they ate and drank and were satisfied. And when it was finished, Almustafa spoke in a vast voice, deep as the sea and full as a great tide under the moon, and he said: "My comrades and my road-fellows, we must needs part this day. Long have we sailed the perilous seas, and we have climbed the steepest mountains and we have wrestled with the storms. We have known hunger, but we have also sat at wedding-feasts. Oftentimes have we been

57

naked, but we have also worn kingly rai-
ment. We have indeed travelled far, but
now we part. Together you shall go your
way, and alone must I go mine.

"And though the seas and the vast lands
shall separate us, still we shall be compan-
ions upon our journey to the Holy Moun-
tain.

"But before we go our severed roads, I
would give unto you the harvest and the
gleaning of my heart:

"Go you upon your way with singing,
but let each song be brief, for only the
songs that die young upon your lips shall
live in human hearts.

"Tell a lovely truth in little words, but
never an ugly truth in any words. Tell the
maiden whose hair shines in the sun that
she is the daughter of the morning. But if
you shall behold the sightless, say not to
him that he is one with night.

"Listen to the flute-player as it were
listening to April, but if you shall hear the
critic and the fault-finder speak, be deaf

as your own bones and as distant as your fancy.

"My comrades and my beloved, upon your way you shall meet men with hoofs; give them of your wings. And men with horns; give them wreaths of laurel. And men with claws; give them petals for fingers. And men with forked tongues; give them honey for words.

"Ay, you shall meet all these and more; you shall meet the lame selling crutches; and the blind, mirrors. And you shall meet the rich men begging at the gate of the Temple.

"To the lame give of your swiftness, to the blind of your vision; and see that you give of yourself to the rich beggars; they are the most needy of all, for surely no man would stretch a hand for alms unless he be poor indeed, though of great possessions.

"My comrades and my friends, I charge you by our love that you be countless paths which cross one another in the desert, where the lions and the rabbits walk, and also the wolves and the sheep.

"And remember this of me: I teach you not giving, but receiving; not denial, but fulfilment; and not yielding, but understanding, with the smile upon the lips.

"I teach you not silence, but rather a song not over-loud.

"I teach you your larger self, which contains all men."

And he rose from the board and went out straightway into the Garden and walked under the shadow of the cypress-trees as the day waned. And they followed him, at a little distance, for their heart was heavy, and their tongue clave to the roof of their mouth.

Only Karima, after she had put by the fragments, came unto him and said: "Master, I would that you suffer me to prepare food against the morrow and your journey."

And he looked upon her with eyes that saw other worlds than this, and he said: "My sister, and my beloved, it is done, even from the beginning of time. The food and the drink is ready, for the morrow, even as for our yesterday and our today.

"I go, but if I go with a truth not yet voiced, that very truth will again seek me and gather me, though my elements be scattered throughout the silences of eternity, and again shall I come before you that I may speak with a voice born anew out of the heart of those boundless silences.

. "And if there be aught of beauty that I have declared not unto you, then once again shall I be called, ay, even by mine own name, Almustafa, and I shall give you a sign, that you may know I have come back to speak all that is lacking, for God will not suffer Himself to be hidden from man, nor His word to lie covered in the abyss of the heart of man.

"I shall live beyond death, and I shall
   sing in your ears
Even after the vast sea-wave carries me
   back

To the vast sea-depth.
I shall sit at your board though without
a body,
And I shall go with you to your fields, a
spirit invisible.
I shall come to you at your fireside, a
guest unseen.
Death changes nothing but the masks
that cover our faces.
The woodsman shall be still a woods-
man,
The ploughman, a ploughman,
And he who sang his song to the wind
shall sing it also to the moving
spheres."

And the disciples were as still as stones,
and grieved in their heart for that he had
said: "I go." But no man put out his hand
to stay the Master, nor did any follow after
his footsteps.

And Almustafa went out from the Gar-
den of his mother, and his feet were swift
and they were soundless; and in a moment,
like a blown leaf in a strong wind, he was

far gone from them, and they saw, as it were, a pale light moving up to the heights.

And the nine walked their ways down the road. But the woman still stood in the gathering night, and she beheld how the light and the twilight were become one; and she comforted her desolation and her aloneness with his words: "I go, but if I go with a truth not yet voiced, that very truth will seek me and gather me, and again shall I come."

And now it was eventide.

And he had reached the hills. His steps had led him to the mist, and he stood among the rocks and the white cypress-trees hidden from all things, and he spoke and said:

"O Mist, my sister, white breath not yet
     held in a mould,
I return to you, a breath white and voice-
     less,
A word not yet uttered.

"O Mist, my wingèd sister mist, we are
     together now,
And together we shall be till life's second
     day,
Whose dawn shall lay you, dewdrops in
     a garden,
And me a babe upon the breast of a
     woman,
And we shall remember.

64

"O Mist, my sister, I come back, a heart
     listening in its depths,
Even as your heart,
A desire throbbing and aimless even as
     your desire,
A thought not yet gathered, even as your
     thought.

"O Mist, my sister, first-born of my mother,
My hands still hold the green seeds you
     bade me scatter,
And my lips are sealed upon the song you
     bade me sing;
And I bring you no fruit, and I bring you
     no echoes,
For my hands were blind, and my lips
     unyielding.

"O Mist, my sister, much did I love the
     world, and the world loved me,
For all my smiles were upon her lips, and
     all her tears were in my eyes.
Yet there was between us a gulf of silence
     which she would not abridge
And I could not overstep.

"O Mist, my sister, my deathless sister
   Mist,
I sang the ancient songs unto my little
   children,
And they listened, and there was wonder-
   ing upon their face;
But tomorrow perchance they will forget
   the song,
And I know not to whom the wind will
   carry the song.
And though it was not mine own, yet it
   came to my heart
And dwelt for a moment upon my lips.

"O Mist, my sister, though all this came to
   pass,
I am at peace.
It was enough to sing to those already
   born.
And though the singing is indeed not
   mine,
Yet it is of my heart's deepest desire.

"O Mist, my sister, my sister Mist,
I am one with you now.

66

No longer am I a self.
The walls have fallen,
And the chains have broken;
I rise to you, a mist,
And together we shall float upon the sea
  until life's second day,
When dawn shall lay you, dewdrops in
  a garden,
And me a babe upon the breast of a
  woman."

Until Lifes second day!

A NOTE ON THE AUTHOR

Kahlil Gibran, poet, philosopher, and artist, was born in 1883 into an affluent and musical Lebanese family. He was a college student in Syria at the age of fifteen, studied art in Paris at the Ecole des Beaux Arts, and had visited America twice before he came to New York to stay in 1912 and adopted English as his literary language. He died in New York City's Greenwich Village on April 10, 1931.

His drawings and paintings have been exhibited in the great capitals of the world and were compared by Auguste Rodin to the work of William Blake. The Prophet, *his most popular book, published in 1923, has been translated into more than twenty languages, and has sold well over a million copies in this country alone.*

A NOTE ON THE TYPE IN WHICH
THIS BOOK IS SET

This book is set (on the linotype) in Original Old Style, of the history of which very little is known; in practically its present form it has been used for many years for fine book and magazine work. The design of its lower-case letters would indicate a derivation from English and Dutch Old Styles of the seventeenth and early eighteenth centuries, the period which reached its culmination in the work of William Caslon. The blackness of its capitals shows clearly, however, that their design was modified in imitation of the Modern faces which so completely displaced the Old Styles during the first half of the nineteenth century. Original Old Style possesses in a high degree those two qualities by which a book type must be judged: first, legibility, and second, the ability to impart a definite character to a page without intruding itself upon the reader's consciousness.

PRINTED AND BOUND BY HADDON CRAFTSMEN,
SCRANTON, PENNSYLVANIA.

BAREFOOT GEN

VOLUME TWO:
THE DAY AFTER

KEIJI NAKAZAWA

Translated by Project Gen

LAST GASP OF SAN FRANCISCO

Barefoot Gen: A Cartoon Story of Hiroshima
Volume Two: The Day After

By Keiji Nakazawa

Published by Last Gasp of San Francisco
777 Florida Street, San Francisco, California, 94110
www.lastgasp.com

First serialized under the title *Hadashi no Gen* in Japan, 1972-3.
Published by Last Gasp with a new translation, 2004.
First hardcover Last Gasp edition, 2016.
ISBN 978-0-86719-832-4

Translation by Project Gen
Volume 2 Translators: Kiyoko Nishita, George Stenson, Alan Gleason,
Jared Cook, Frederik Schodt.

Project Gen Volunteers: Namie Asazuma, Kazuko Futakuchi, Michael
Gordon, Kyoko Honda, Yukari Kimura, Nobutoshi Kohara, Nante Kotta,
Michiko Tanaka, Kazuko Yamada.

Edited by Alan Gleason and Colin Turner
Production: Colin Turner
Cover design: Evan Hayden

Printed in China by Prolong Press Ltd.

For more information visit www.barefootgen.net

Barefoot Gen: Comics After the Bomb

An Introduction by Art Spiegelman

Gen haunts me. The first time I read it was in the late 1970s, shortly after I'd begun working on *Maus*, my own extended comic-book chronicle of the twentieth century's other central cataclysm. I had the flu at the time and read it while high on fever. *Gen* burned its way into my heated brain with all the intensity of a fever-dream. I've found myself remembering images and events from the *Gen* books with a clarity that made them seem like mem-ories from my own life, rather than Nakazawa's. I will never forget the people dragging their own melted skin as they walk through the ruins of Hiroshima, the panic-stricken horse on fire galloping through the city, the maggots crawling out of the sores of a young girl's ruined face. *Gen* deals with the trauma of the atom bomb without flinching. There are no irradiated Godzillas or super-mutants, only tragic realities. I've just reread the books recently and I'm glad to discover that the vividness of *Barefoot Gen* emanates from the work itself and not simply from my fever. Or, more accurately, it emanates from something intrinsic to the comics medium itself and from the events Nakazawa lived through and depicted.

Comics are a highly charged medium, delivering densely con-centrated information in relatively few words and simplified code-images. It seems to me that this is a model of how the brain for-mulates thoughts and remembers. We think in cartoons. Comics have often demonstrated how well suited they are to telling action adventure stories or jokes, but the small scale of the images and the directness of a medium that has something in common with handwriting allow comics a kind of intimacy that also make them surprisingly well suited to autobiography.

It's odd that, until the development of underground comics in the late 1960s, overtly autobiographical comics have not com-prised an important "genre." Rarer still are works that overtly grapple with the intersection between personal history and world history. Perhaps it was necessary to have a concept of comics as suitable adult fare for the medium to move toward autobiography. Or so I thought until I became more aware of Keiji Nakazawa's career. In 1972 Nakazawa, then 33, wrote and drew a directly autobiographical account of surviving the atomic blast at Hiroshima for a Japanese children's comic weekly. It was called, with chilling directness, "I Saw It." A year later he began his *Gen* series, a slightly fictionalized narrative also based on having seen "It," an adventure story of a boy caught in hell, a "Disasters of War" with speech balloons.

In Japan there is no stigma attached to reading comics; they're consumed in truly astonishing numbers (some comics weeklies have been known to sell over 3 million copies of a single issue) by all classes and ages. There are comics devoted to economic theory, mah jongg, and male homosexual love stories designed for pre-pubescent girls, as well as more familiar tales of samurai, robots and mutants. However, I should confess to a very limited knowledge of Japanese comics. They form a vast unexplored universe only tangentially connected to my own. Sometimes that seems true of everything about Japan, and *Gen* may be an ideal starting point for the twain to meet.

The modern comic book is a specifically Western form (making it all the more appropriate as a medium for reporting on the horrors brought to the East by the atom bomb), but Japanese comics have stylistic quirks and idioms that are quite different from ours, and these must be learned and accepted as part of the process of reading *Gen*. The stories are often quite long (the entire *Gen* saga reportedly runs to close on 2,000 pages), usually with rather few words on a page, allowing an entire 200-page book to be read during a short commuter ride. Overt symbolism is characteristic of Japanese comics; for Nakazawa it takes the form of a relentlessly reappearing sun that glares implacably through the pages. It is the marker of time passing, the giver of life, the flag of Japan, and a metronome that gives rhythm to Gen's story.

The degree of casual violence in Japanese comics is typically far greater than in our homegrown products. Gen's pacifist father freely wallops his kids with a frequency and force that we might easily perceive as criminal child abuse rather than the sign of affection that is intended. The sequence of Gen brawling with the chairman's son and literally biting his fingers off is (forgive me, I can't resist) especially hard to swallow. Yet these casual small-scale brutalities pale to naturalistic proportions when compared to the enormity of dropping a nuclear weapon on a civilian population.

The physiognomy of the characters often leans to the cloyingly cute, with special emphasis on Disney-like oversized Caucasian eyes and generally neotenic faces. Nakazawa is hardly the worst offender, though his cartoon style derives from that tradition. His draftsmanship is somewhat graceless, even homely, and without much nuance, but it gets the job done. It is clear and efficient, and it performs the essential magic trick of all good narrative art: the characters come to living, breathing life. The drawing's greatest virtue is its straightforward, blunt sincerity. Its conviction and honesty allow you to believe in the unbelievable and impossible things that did, indeed, happen in Hiroshima. It is the inexorable art of the witness.

Although the strangeness of the unfamiliar idioms and conventions of Japanese comics language may set up a hurdle for the Western reader first confronted with this book, it also offers one of its central pleasures. Nakazawa is an exceptionally skillful storyteller who knows how to keep his reader's attention in order to tell the Grim Things That Must Be Told. He effortlessly communicates a wealth of information about day-to-day life in wartime Japan and the anatomy of survival without slowing down the trajectory of his narrative. There is a paradox inherent in talking about such pleasures in the context of a work that illuminates the reality of mass death, yet the exposure to another culture's frame of reference, the sympathetic identification one develops with the protagonists and the very nature of narrative itself are all intrinsically pleasurable. Arguably, by locating the causes of the bombings exclusively in the evils of Japanese militaristic nationalism rather than in the *Realpolitik* of Western racism and cold-war power-jockeying, Nakazawa may make the work a little *too* pleasurable for American and British readers.

Ultimately, *Gen* is a very optimistic work. Nakazawa believes that his story can have a cautionary effect, that mankind can be improved to the point of acting in its own genuine self-interest. Indeed, Gen is a plucky little hero, embodying such virtues as loyalty, bravery, and industriousness. Nakazawa's faith in the possibility for Goodness may mark the work in some cynical eyes as true Literature for Children, but the underlying fact is that the artist is reporting on his own survival — not simply on the *events* that he lived through, but on the philosophical/psychological basis for that survival. His work is humanistic and humane, demonstrating and stressing the necessity for empathy among humans if we're to survive into another century.

A Note from the Author

Keiji Nakazawa

The atomic bomb exploded 600 meters above my hometown of Hiroshima on August 6, 1945 at 8:15 a.m. I was a little over a kilometer away from the epicenter, standing at the back gate of Kanzaki Primary School, when I was hit by a terrible blast of wind and searing heat. I was six years old. I owe my life to the school's concrete wall. If I hadn't been standing in its shadow, I would have been burned to death instantly by the 5,000-degree heat flash. Instead, I found myself in a living hell, the details of which remain etched in my brain as if it happened yesterday.

My mother, Kimiyo, was eight months pregnant. She was on the second floor balcony of our house, had just finished hanging up the wash to dry, and was turning to go back inside when the bomb exploded. The blast blew the entire balcony, with my mother on it, into the alley behind our house. Miraculously, my mother survived without a scratch.

The blast blew our house flat. The second floor collapsed onto the first, trapping my father, my sister Eiko, and my brother Susumu under it. My brother had been sitting in the front doorway, playing with a toy ship. His head was caught under the rafter over the doorway. He frantically kicked his legs and cried out for my mother. My father, trapped inside the house, begged my mother to do something. My sister had been crushed by a rafter and killed instantly.

My mother frantically tried to lift the rafters off them, but she wasn't strong enough to do it by herself. She begged passersby to stop and help, but nobody would. In that atomic hell, people could only think of their own survival; they had no time for anyone else. My mother tried everything she could, but to no avail. Finally, in despair, she sat down in the doorway, clutching my crying brother and helplessly pushing at the rafter that was crushing him.

The fires that followed the blast soon reached our house. It was quickly enveloped in flame. My brother yelled that he was burning; my father kept begging my mother to get some help. My mother, half-mad with grief and desperation, sobbed that she would stay and die with them. But our next-door neighbor found my mother just in time and dragged her away.

For the rest of her days, my mother never forgot the sound of the voices of her husband and son, crying out for her to save them. The shock sent my mother into labor, and she gave birth to a daughter by the side of the road that day. She named the baby Tomoko. But Tomoko died only four months later -- perhaps from malnutrition, perhaps from radiation sickness, we didn't know.

After escaping the flames near the school, I found my mother there by the roadside with her newborn baby. Together we sat and watched the scenes of hell unfolding around us.

My father had been a painter of lacquer work and traditional-style Japanese painting. He was also a member of an anti-war theater group that performed plays like Gorky's "The Lower Depths." Eventually the thought police arrested the entire troupe and put them in the Hiroshima Prefectural Prison. My father was held there for a year and a half. Even when I was a young child, my father constantly told me that Japan had been stupid and reckless to start the war.

Thanks, no doubt, to my father's influence, I enjoyed drawing from an early age. After the war I began reading Osamu Tezuka's comic magazine *Shin-Takarajima* (*New Treasure Island*); that had a huge impact on me. I began slavishly copying Tezuka's drawings and turned into a manga maniac. Hiroshima was an empty, burnt-out wasteland and we went hungry every day, but when I drew comics, I was happy and forgot everything else. I vowed early on to become a professional cartoonist when I grew up.

In 1961 I pursued my dream by moving to Tokyo. A year later I published my first cartoon serial in the manga monthly *Shonen Gaho* (*Boys' Pictorial*). From then on I was a full-time cartoonist.

In 1966, after seven years of illness, my mother died in the A-Bomb Victims Hospital in Hiroshima. When I went to the crematorium to collect her ashes, I was shocked. There were no bones left in my mother's ashes, as there normally are after a cremation. Radioactive cesium from the bomb had eaten away at her bones to the point that they disintegrated. The bomb had even deprived me of my mother's bones. I was overcome with rage. I vowed that I would never forgive the Japanese militarists who started the war, nor the Americans who had so casually dropped the bomb on us.

I began drawing comics about the A-bomb as a way to avenge my mother. I vented my anger through a "Black" series of six manga published in an adult manga magazine, starting with *Kuroi Ame ni Utarete* (*Struck by Black Rain*). Then I moved to *Shukan Shonen Jump* (*Weekly Boys' Jump*), where I began a series of works about the war and the A-bomb starting with *Aru Hi Totsuzen ni* (*One Day, Suddenly*). When the monthly edition of *Jump* launched a series of autobiographical works by its cartoonists, I was asked to lead off with my own story. My 45-page manga autobiography was titled *Ore wa Mita* (*I Saw It*). My editor at *Jump*, Tadasu Nagano, commenting that I must have more to say that wouldn't fit in 45 pages, urged me to draw a longer series based on my personal experiences. I gratefully began the series right away. That was in 1972.

I named my new story *Hadashi no Gen* (*Barefoot Gen*). The young protagonist's name, Gen, has several meanings in Japanese. It can mean the "root" or "origin" of something, but also "elemental" in the sense of an atomic element, as well as a "source" of vitality and happiness. I envisioned Gen as barefoot, standing firmly atop the burnt-out rubble of Hiroshima, raising his voice against war and nuclear weapons. Gen is my alter ego, and his family is just like my own. The episodes in *Barefoot Gen* are all based on what really happened to me or to other people in Hiroshima.

Human beings are foolish. Thanks to bigotry, religious fanaticism, and the greed of those who traffic in war, the Earth is never at peace, and the specter of nuclear war is never far away. I hope that Gen's story conveys to its readers the preciousness of peace and the courage we need to live strongly, yet peacefully. In *Barefoot Gen*, wheat appears as a symbol of that strength and courage. Wheat pushes its shoots up through the winter frost, only to be trampled again and again. But the trampled wheat sends strong roots into the earth and grows straight and tall. And one day, that wheat bears fruit.

BAREFOOT GEN

THE DAY AFTER

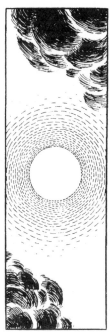

Groan...

Water...

Look, Mama. Those people's skin is hanging down.

This was no ordinary bomb.

Charge! Charge! I'm an army general. Charge!

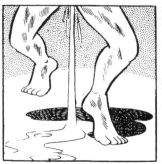

Charge! Charge!

What's wrong with him? He's crazy...

1

STAGGER

M-Ma'am...

Yes?

I'm Setsuko Ohkawa... first grade, Daiichi Girls' School... If my parents are alive, please tell them I died here...

What are you saying?! You mustn't give up!

My... parents are Hirokichi Ohkawa and Miyo...

Gasp... I want to see my mom... I want to see my dad...

FLOP

Hey! Hang on!

S-she's dead...

Poor girl... Bury her, Gen, will you?

Ah... It hurts! Kill me, please kill me!

Water! Water, please!

Ah! Water! Water!

2

Look, Gen, there are so many piles of bodies all over the city... I wonder how many people have died... Hiroshima has become a living hell.

The rotting bodies smell awful. It's making me sick.

I wish I could've done something for them, but there're no doctors or medicine around.

It's the Americans' fault! Why'd they drop this horrible bomb?

We were lucky to survive.

How did you escape being hurt?

I was hanging the clothes on the laundry pole and was blown down.

Maybe the roof blocked the blast from me...

Your father, Eiko and Shinji were in the house. They were crushed under the fallen roof...

I could have saved them if only Ryukichi and his father had helped me... To hell with them...

3

How did you survive the bomb, Gen?

The concrete school wall behind me blocked the blast.

The lady in front of me was burned to death. Her body was so badly burnt...

What a horrible blast that was...

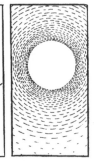

You have a burn mark on your head.

Do I? No wonder it hurts.

What're we going to do, Mama?

Your brother Koji may come back. So let's wait here for a while.

The city of Hiroshima had disappeared, buried under cries of pain and piles of corpses. The U.S. announced that the destruction of Hiroshima was caused by an atomic bomb, and urged Japan to unconditionally surrender...

But Japan's war leaders feared that panic might spread among the people. They hid the truth about the bomb and insisted that the war go on...

防火用水

Sign: Water for fire

Knowing that Japan had no intention of surrendering, the U.S. dropped a second atomic bomb nicknamed "Fat Man" on the city of Nagasaki at 11:05 a.m., August 9. It was three days after the bombing of Hiroshima.

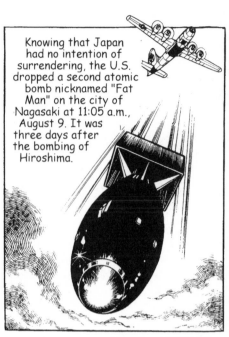

And in Nagasaki, too, tens of thousands of citizens writhed in pain and died...

ROAR

As it has always been, it is the powerless, nameless, ordinary people who die in wars waged by a handful of men in power...

It hurts!

Water... give me some water.

Water, please!

On the same day, August 9, the Soviet Union attacked the Japanese Kwantung Army, breaking the Japan-USSR Non-Aggression Treaty.

Terrified by the atomic bombs and shaken by the USSR's entry into the war, Japan's leaders finally saw there was no way out and began to consider unconditional surrender...

.....

Every-
thing is
gone...

Everything
has
disappeared...

What will
become
of us?

What
should
we do?
Tell me,
Papa...

Survive, Gen!
Be brave and
take good care
of your mother!

All right,
I will.
I will,
Papa.

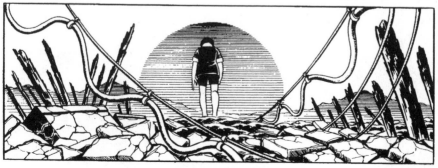

Honkawa
Elementary School

Ohta River

Aioi Bridge

Chamber of
Commerce and Industr

Motoyasu River

Motoyasu
Bridge

Ground Zero:
A-bomb Dome
shima Industrial
omotion Hall)

TAP TAP

Ah!

Hee
hee!

P-Papa!
Eiko!
Shinji!

Hey, Gen! What're
you so glum about?
Cheer up! Cheer up!

Wha...?! You're all alive! Am I dreaming...?

RUB RUB

We managed to get out of the house when it burned down, Gen.

Y-you aren't ghosts, are you?...

What are you talking about? Look! I have legs!

Me, too, Gen.

We're alive, Gen.

Wow! Papa, Eiko, Shinji, you're all alive!

Yay! I'm so happy, Shinji! So happy!

Yeah! Isn't it great, Gen!

Hurray!

Hurray!

I'll hurry to tell Mama. She'll be so surprised she might faint!

Come on, Shinji. We have a baby sister. She's cute!

·····

What are you doing? Come on now!

We have something to do first, Gen. We'll come later.

What is it, Papa?

We want to find something for the baby.

You don't have to bring anything.

No. We have to. I'll find a pretty kimono for her!

Gen, I'll find something tasty for her, too. Wait for me!

Hey, Papa, Eiko, Shinji! I'll go with you. Wait up!

Hey! Wait up!

Don't leave me alone!

No! Papa! Eiko! Shinji! Wait up!

Gen... Gen!

GASP!

What's the matter, Gen? You were crying. Were you having a nightmare...?

Was I dreaming?...

Mama, I just had a dream where Papa, Eiko and Shinji came back to us safe and sound.

They might be alive, Mama!

.....

They might come back here with gifts for the baby.

How wonderful it would be if your dream were true...

It IS true! I'm sure it's true!

I believe my dream!

13

Thinking about it makes me happy, Mama.

Wow, I can hardly wait for them to come home!

Stop thinking about such things. Give them up, Gen...

.....

You saw them dying in the fire...

They're dead...

SHIVER

No! No!.

They're all alive. Papa, Eiko and Shinji will be back here with gifts for the baby!

Don't say they're dead, Mama! Don't! Don't!

WAH! WAH! WAH!

.....

SOB

14

Gen!

I'm sorry, Gen. I tried to destroy your dream...

I was wrong. They're alive. I'm sure they are...

Yes, let's believe, and be happy, Gen!

Water...

Sob...

WAH! WAH! WAH!

Are you hungry, little one?

WAH! WAH! WAH!

Here you go.

WAH! WAH!

SLURP

WAH! WAH! WAH!

What's wrong?

15

WAH! WAH!

Why is she crying?

There's no milk coming from my breasts, Gen.

What!

No wonder... We haven't eaten anything for the past three days...

WAH! WAH!

W-what should I do? She'll die if I can't feed her...

No, Mama! Don't let her die!

Rice... I need rice...

Can rice help her?

Rice dumplings are said to increase a mother's milk.

And we can use rice broth as a substitute for milk...

WAH! WAH!

But it's impossible to get rice... Everything has been burned down... What can we do?

WAH! WAH! WAH! WAH! WAH!

To find rice, we'll have to go way out into the countryside.

Mama, I'll go. I'll go anywhere to get rice for her!

WAH! WAH!

16

Wait here till I come back, Mama.

W-will you be all right, Gen?

Sure I will! I won't let my sister die.

I have to show her to Papa, Eiko and Shinji when they come back.

Hey, sis, you may be hungry but you have to hang on. I'll bring lots of rice for you. OK? Don't die. I won't forgive you if you die!

I'll be back soon, Mama.

Gen, be care-ful.

.....

Dear, Gen has become a strong young man... You can be proud of him.

17

Somebody, please give my baby some milk.

Water... Water...

SLURP SLURP

WAH! WAH! WAH!

Excuse me, would you please give some milk to my baby?

WAH! WAH!

What?! I don't even have enough milk for my own baby. How can I feed yours?

Ask somebody else.

Y-you won't?

WAH! WAH!

There, there. Please don't cry like that.

18

GOO GOO

I'll ask her...

Excuse me, will you please breast-feed my baby? Please.

Hello?

THUD

She's dead!

Her baby doesn't even know she's dead... Poor little boy...

GOO GOO

Oh, I know you're hungry... Please don't cry...

WAH! WAH!

If only I could feed her...

WAH! WAH! WAH!

Gen, bring some rice back soon... or she'll starve to death...

19

This work is endless. There's bodies everywhere.

We better burn them quick. They stink like hell. They're rotting already.

Hurry it up, Sergeant Ogawa. Clear the bodies faster!

Yes, sir.

It smells awful.

Ugh! They're just like fish laid out in the fish market.

Ah!

Hey soldier, he's still alive. He's moving his mouth!

Forget it! He'll die sooner or later.

Scram, kid! You're in our way!

B-but he's still alive...

Up you go.

This truck is full. We can't fit any more.

OK. Let's haul 'em to the fire!

How many people have died from the bomb...? There's too many to count!

What're you doing?

It's a dead Yankee. He was in the POW camp in Hiroshima.

You bastard!

Dirty rat!

Hit him!

This is all his fault!

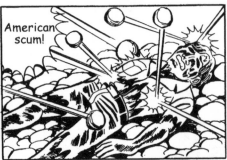

Bastard! Here, throw a rock yourself.

American scum!

WOBBLE

Can I join in, boys?

Yeah. Come on, ma'am. Be our guest.

You evil Yankee! American pig!

Take THIS for my dear husband. He was crushed under our house.

And this one is for my daughter. She died with all her skin burnt off.

THIS is for my poor grandson. He was burned to death in the fire...

You damn Yankee!

You took them all from me! Give me back my husband, my daughter, my grandson, my home!

Why? Why did you drop that horrible bomb on us?

We didn't do anything to you. Why do we have to suffer like this?

SOB...

MOAN....

The Americans even killed their own soldiers. They really are evil...

But I can't waste any more time. I've gotta hurry and bring some rice home, or our baby'll die.

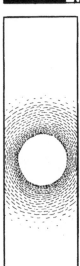

PANT... PANT...

WOBBLE

I'm starting to feel sick!

Pant pant... I'm getting dizzy... Must be from not eating... and the smell from those rotting bodies...

Oh, no.

I'm gonna faint...

WOBBLE

No! I have to be strong. If I don't bring any rice back, our baby will die.

Unhh... Everything's going black!

H-help, Mama!

THUD!

URKK

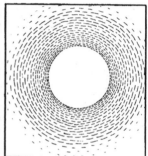

TROMP TROMP

Hey, there's one more body over there.

He's in better shape than most of 'em.

25

Hurry. Pile these bodies up, pour the gasoline on and burn 'em.

重油

重油

Oof.

Is this one really dead? Looks like he might be alive.

There's something strange about the bomb they dropped here. Some people seem fine but then they suddenly drop dead. Why is that?

I don't know.

Perhaps he's one of them.

Poor kid...

26

SPLOOSH
SPLOOSH
SPLOOSH

OK.
Here
we go.

ROAR!

Namu
Amida
Butsu...

Namu
Amida
Butsu.*

* Buddhist prayer

27

Namu Amida Butsu. Namu Amida Butsu.

AIEEE!

Ah!

Wha-?

Aaghh!

Hey! That boy's alive!

Yow! I'm burning! Help!

Aiee!

Quick! Put out the fire.

28

Hey kid, you OK? We thought you were dead.

GROAN

You idiots! I'm alive. How could you mistake me for dead...?

I- I'm sorry.

Stupid! Saying sorry doesn't help!

You're burned. I'll take you to the Medical Station.

It's a good thing you came to. In another moment you would have been with those burning bodies.

CRACKLE

B-burning flesh smells awful...

Let's go.

29

Ow! My burns hurt!

Hang on, kid. Here, eat this. It's my lunch.

Wow! Bis-cuits!

Y-yummy!

Mmm, it tastes great! I haven't eaten in three days, you know.

Yeah?... You can have 'em all. Eat as many as you like.

Really? But then you'll have nothing to eat.

Don't worry. I haven't felt like eating much these past few days.

Gee, thanks, soldier!

I have a boy like you in Kumamoto.

Carrying you on my back like this reminds me of my son.

30

I'll sing for you, kid, so cheer up...

.....

I can hardly wait for the day when my servant days are over... ♪ ♪

Oh, how I want to go home... ♪

Soldier, there're dead bodies in every water tank. They've swollen up like watermelons...

Poor things...

The fire must've been so hot. They had nowhere else to run but into these small tanks...

Look. This woman was trying to save her children by holding them tight. But all in vain...

防火用水

That's a boy and his little sister. He was trying to protect her.

Cruel... It's just too cruel...

.....

Hey, soldier, you get those Yankees, OK? You've gotta win this war!

It's too awful, the way these people died!

I-I'll get 'em, son.

They killed so many innocent women and children...

You get 'em, sir. You show 'em.

.....

Hey, what happened? You messed your pants!

Nonsense! Why would I do that?!

You mean you didn't notice?

S-stop fooling with me, kid...

I'm not lying. See for yourself.

What?

He...he's right. When did I...

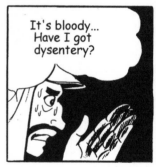

It's bloody... Have I got dysentery?

S-strange. I don't have any pain in my stomach...

Hey, your hair just fell out!

My hair...?

34

T-this much hair at one time...

Wha-what's happening to me...?

Ha ha! You have lots of bald spots on your head!

GRRR...

S-sorry I laughed at you, mister...

BRRR BRRR

I-I'm cold...

Cold? It's the middle of summer. You feel cold?!

Agh, I'm f-freezing!!

BRRR

Please help me, son...

T-take it easy, mister. What's wrong?

Blankets. Get me some blankets.

Where? Everything's been burned.

I-I'm so cold... Please, put something over me...

Oh no! What'll I do?

!

Hey, how about this sheet of tin?

Ow!!

Wow, the sun sure heated this up.

Maybe it'll keep him warm.

36

Get a hold of yourself, soldier!

Are you still cold?

Yes, I'm f-freezing. P-put more on me...

How can he feel cold with that hot tin on him?

OOF!

URGHH

He must have gone crazy!

Groan... Ryota, Shinkichi... Your dad is home with lots of presents for you, boys...

He must have a fever. He's dreaming about his family.

37

 Hang on, soldier! Your kids will cry if you die!

Moan...

 If I leave him here, he'll die... I'll take him to the Medical Station.

Hold on! I'll take you to the doctor.

 THUD

Argh!

 He's too heavy to carry on my back.

What'll I do?!

 Ahh... Ungh...

 I know! I can make a sled out of this tin sheet.

 How did I get myself into this...

Now it's ready.

Hey, am I smart or what!

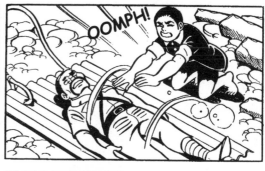
OOMPH!

You've gotta hang on, OK?

Ah... Ah...

Heave-ho. Heave-ho.

This isn't fair! I was the one who was supposed to be taken to the doctor.

RATTLE RATTLE

RATTLE RATTLE RATTLE

Heave-ho. Heave-ho.

It hurts...
Help!
Give me water...
Groan...

It hurts so much, Nurse. Please, give me some medicine, now!

I'm sorry, we can't. We've run out of medicine.

Only treat the ones who look like they might live, Nurse.

Yes, Doctor.

Hurry, please. Get this glass out of my body. The pieces are scraping together inside me! It hurts so much!

My wounds are rotting, and they're full of maggots... I can't stand the itch...

Somebody help me...

Sign: Medical Station

41

Same as those soldiers over there. They came here to help clear out the bodies in the city. They came here healthy and now they're dead...

W-what happened?

☆ I have no idea.

Maybe it was that new atomic bomb they dropped on Hiroshima.

A-atomic bomb!?

No! I can't stand it!

I brought you all the way here for nothing!

Open your eyes, soldier... You can't just die.

Sing me a song again.

Get well and go back to your boys in Kumamoto.

Aagh, this is too much!

Why is everybody around me dying?

I don't want to see any more dead bodies.

Those damn Americans! Why did they have to drop such a horrible bomb?

Somebody, please nurse my baby.

.....

WAH! WAH!

Why? Why is everybody dying?!

Shut up! That baby will die soon anyway!

H...how could you say such a thing?

Name tag: Gen Nakaoka, Grade 2

Die! Die!

A...are you crazy?

Give it to me! I'll kill it!

Stop! What are you doing?!

Here. Die! Die!

SLURP SLURP SLURP

Y... You're...

.....

43

Ah. Here you go. Drink till you're full, dear.

W...what in the world is she...

Don't worry. I won't kill your child.

A few minutes ago, I was nursing my own baby.

But now he's... he's...

Look. He was burned and died covered with maggots.

When I saw your baby, I was so sad and jealous that I felt like killing her... That's why I talked that way.

I...I was stupid.

M... ma'am.

But don't worry. I'll feed her as if she were my own.

Thank you so much. You've saved her.

You don't have to thank me... I can forget my sorrows for a while by helping.

.....

44

SLURP SLURP

L...lucky little one! You're so lucky.

Gen! Your sister will survive. This lady saved her.

Puff puff... Gotta get out to the country and bring back some rice, or my sister will die. Mama's waiting!

I lost a lot of time trying to help that soldier. I've gotta hurry.

Oh!

M...my hair is...falling out, too...

L... lots of it...

BRRR

Eee! Just like that soldier...

45

Agh! A-am I dying, too?!

No! No!

I don't wanna die!

H...help me, Mama, help me. I'm scared!

The atomic bomb not only destroyed Hiroshima, but spread radiation throughout the city. The radiation quietly ate into the bodies of healthy people... and began to destroy their cells. It was the beginning of the A-bomb disease, the terrifying radiation sickness that still affects many people...

Beggars from eight hundred provinces
Stand with their bowls at the gate...
Hey, Mister!
Give us some food!
Give us enough to fill our bellies!

PO-PO-POTATO
SWEET POTATO
HEY!

Boy! I've found a nice cap.

It's a firefighter's!

Go tell everyone that Fire Chief Gen will put out all the fires!

47

BRRR

M...my hair is all gone! I'm bald...

After the soldier lost his hair, he died...

No!

Damn it!
SPLASH

I'm not going to die. I'm not!

I'm healthy. I'm strong! I am!

I won't die. No way!

I don't care if I've gone bald! See if I care!

Po-po-potato! Sweet potato!

Oh, it's 4:30 in the morning
Daddy walks out the door
With his lunchbox full of cheap noodles
Yes, it's a hard life for poor folks
Day in, day out,
the fleas keep biting...

Pant pant...

I don't want to die.

I don't want to die.

Wah! Please don't let me die!

WAH! WAH! WAH!

POP
POP

W-
what's
that
sound?

POP

Ack!

POP

T-the bellies of those
bodies are swollen up
like balloons...
Their guts have rotted
and the gas is bursting
out of them...

Ecchh...
it
stinks!

POP

POP

POP

51

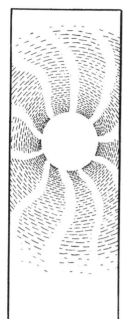

Whew. It sure is hot.

The sun is so bright...

STAGGER

Pant pant... I'll take a rest in that streetcar.

Wow. The blast blew this big streetcar all the way over here...

Puff puff...

Huh?

W-what are these things crawling on me?

M... maggots!

Why are there so many maggots here?

Urk!

54

Ugh! This car is full of bodies with maggots all over them!

This man is dead but still holding the strap.

The bomb must have killed them all in an instant...

Agh, that smell...

I can't stand it...

URGH!

I can't take any more of this!

The smell is making me dizzy...

55

Puff puff... With all these bodies everywhere, I can't find a place to rest.

BZZZ

BZZZ

W-what's that sound?

Ow! ZAP ZAP

ZAP ZAP

ZAP ZAP

BZZZZZ

Aaahh! Something's coming after me!

BZZZZ

Aagh!

BZZZZ

Aargh! They... they're flies!

Flies from all the dead bodies are swarming all over me!

Ouch! They're flying right into my eyes!

Oh, no. They're crawling into my ears!

Damn you! Get off me!

Go away! Shoo!

Filthy flies! They won't go away.

Get off me!

Damn you!

Yaahh! Help!

BZZZ

BZZZ

Gasp...

This is scary!

Pant pant... This heat is making all the maggots turn into flies right away...

Ah!

BZZZ   BZZZ

Mumble...
Mumble...

BZZZ

W-what's the matter with that lady...?

How can she stand all those flies on her?

Mumble...
Mumble...

Maybe she's too tired to shoo them away.

Poor woman! I'll help her.

Get out, flies! Go away! Scram!

59

WHOOSH

BZZZZ

You fool! What are you doing?!

Huh?

Stop it right now!

I-I was trying to help you...

How could you chase my precious flies away? Idiot!

SLAP!

Ow!

Y-you old witch! How come you hit me?

Now come back, my dear Shotaro.

Is...is she crazy?

BZZZZ

60

I can't believe this...

I'm sorry I hit you, boy...

But these flies are the reincarnation of my only son, Shotaro...

T-they are?

Look. Maggots are coming out of Shotaro's body and changing into flies.

The flies come to me just as Shotaro used to... I can hear him calling, "Mother! Mother!"...

61

I feel comforted with these flies around me....

.....

Ah... He was a tender-hearted boy and was always nice to me.

He just happened to be in Hiroshima to visit a relative and...

Here, Shotaro. I've brought you some peaches from our garden... The peaches you liked so much.

Here, eat...

Is it good, Shotaro?

I have lots, so eat as many as you like...

You too, young man.

Wow! You'll let me have one? Gee, thanks, ma'am!

I'm sorry I called you an old witch. I-I didn't realize...

62

Ah... I don't know how I will live from now on...

My husband was killed in battle and now Shotaro, my only son, my only hope, is dead too. I have nobody to live for...

Only three days ago, Shotaro left home with a big smile on his face...

Call to your mother just once more, Shotaro.

Please. Please.

Ah, Shotaro, Shotaro...

.....

Come on, ma'am. You've got to be strong.

Sob... Sob...

I-I've gotta go now.

I have to get some rice for my mother.

I know it's hard for you, ma'am, but hang in there, OK? I gotta go...

That's enough... I've seen too many bodies. I want to get out of here.

Boy! This peach looks delicious.

.....

W-wait! I'd better keep this for Mama. If she eats it, maybe she can feed the baby...

Pant pant...

Wait for me, Mama. I'll bring some rice back for you.

Ah!

64

T- that's my sister!

The way she walks... the way she looks... It's got to be Eiko!

S-she's alive. I knew it!

Papa and Shinji must be alive, too.

EIKO!

Eiko! Eiko!

65

That's Eiko for sure.

She looks just like that from behind. I know it's her.

Eiko's alive! My sister's alive!

I knew it! I knew it! They're all alive!

Eiko!

Eiko!

WAIT! HEY! WAIT UP!

Pant pant...

Eiko!

66

WAH! Eiko, I'm so glad you're alive. I knew you weren't dead!

Mama's alive too!

And we have a baby sister now!

Eiko...?

Gasp!

.....

I'm not Eiko!

My name is Natsue!

67

Y-you're not Eiko...?

You're not my sister?

WAH!

I want to see my sister! I want to see my brother Shinji! I want to see Papa!

WAH! WAH! WAH!

.....

SLAP!

Don't be a crybaby!

Get hold of yourself!

B... but...

I hate crybabies...

Sniff... From the back, she looks just like Eiko...

68

What's she doing? She's looking into the mouths of dead people...

Not this one...

WOBBLE

She's acting weird.

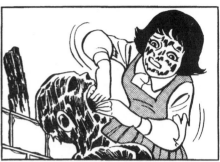

Not this one, either...

W-what are you doing?!

I've looked in hundreds of mouths, but I haven't found her yet.

My mother has three gold-capped teeth in front and three in the back.

Where can she be?

You're looking for your mother's body...?

Don't worry about me... I'll be going to meet your dear departed father... Leave now, and save yourself...

No! Don't be a fool, mother!

Please stand up! Come with me!

I can't... It's no use. But promise me, Natsue, you'll bury me next to your father...

Mother! You can't die!

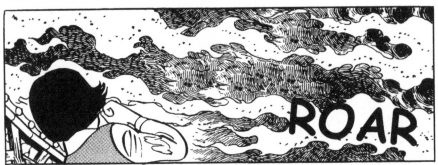

ROAR

Aahh! The flames are coming together from all sides! They're covering everything!

Eek!

KRRAAKK

Aiee!

MOTHER!

.....

.....

I promised her I'd bury her ashes with Father's. I've got to find her body if it's the last thing I do.

Sob... She really loved Japanese dance. She wanted to see me become a professional and dance on a big stage...

She's a dancer? Poor girl... With those burns, she'll never be able to dance in public.

73

Now she'll never see me dance again...

I can't even find her...

Sob...

Don't cry Natsue. I'll help you look for her.

Why are you being so nice to me?

B-because you remind me of my sister Eiko.

We'll look for her together... OK?

T...thank you. I appreciate that.

Agh! My face itches!

It itches so bad, I can't stand it! Is my face all right?

Uh...

Something's moving...

POP

POP

SPLAT

Ack!

Yuck! I just touched her face and pus shot out!

How is my face? I want to know.

.....

Hey, do you have a mirror?

N-no.

Tell me, do I look pretty?

Y... yeah.

Am I pretty, really? Don't lie to me.

Y...yes, you are. You've got a slight burn, though.

Oh, that's a relief! If my face were ugly, I'd kill myself.

.....

Because then I couldn't dance in public...

Dance is my life...

Now, let's look for your mother.

Y-yeah...

Pant pant...

Pant pant...

It's no use... We've looked all over, but we can't find her...

78

Ahh, where can she be?

Mother, you fool! Don't hide! Where are you?!

She's probably somewhere under the rubble, Natsue.

Urk!

Oh no! Black blood!

A-are you all right, Natsue?

Groan...

Gasp... I can't breathe.... Water...

Hang on, Natsue!

Water... Get me water...

Where am I going to find water around here...?

Oh!

I was going to give this peach to Mama...

but I'll give it to her...

I'm sorry, Mama. I won't be giving this to you.

Just imagine that I'm giving it to Eiko...

Eat this, Natsue.

A-a peach!!

GOBBLE

Oh... It tastes so good...

Gulp.

Gasp... T-thanks, kid...

I'll never forget you... I know you must have wanted that peach for yourself...

It's OK, Natsue.

Pant pant... I'm t-tired... I'll just stay here...

No! Come on, you've got to get up!

You're better off not worrying about me.

No! If I leave you here, you might die!

Die? No, I'm not going to die!
Not before I become
a famous dancer!

THUD

Natsue!

Moan...

She fainted.
Wow, she has
a really high
fever!

What's the
matter? She has
purple spots all
over her body.

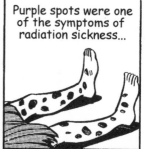

Purple spots were one
of the symptoms of
radiation sickness...

I can't let
her die...

It's as if my own
sister Eiko were
dying. I've got to help
her! What'll I do...?

VROOOMM

81

SCREECH!

All injured persons, board this truck! We'll take you to the Army Hospital in Ninoshima!

All injured persons, board this truck!

Great! I'll ask them to take her to the hospital.

Hold on, Natsue. I'll get them to take care of you.

Ah...

Wait up, soldiers, wait up!

Come on, hurry up! We haven't got all day.

Groan...

Oh, all right, here, I'll help you up.

Agh! His flesh came right off in my hands! No use carrying this one.

H-how aw-ful!

Take her to the hospital, please.

OK. Get on.

There you are, now.

Pant pant...

83

84

Ahh...

Groan...

It hurts...

Water... Water...

Help...

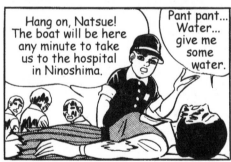

Hang on, Natsue! The boat will be here any minute to take us to the hospital in Ninoshima.

Pant pant... Water... give me some water.

She wants water, too... All the burned people ask for water...

H-hurry. I need water... My throat's on fire...

O-OK. I'll go get some!

Water, water, water... I've got to find something to put it in.

85

Aha!

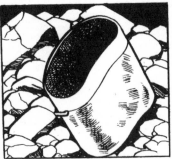

Just what I need! A mess kit!

Ack! There's a hand stuck to the handle!

Hey! Let go!

FWISSHH

Wow! I found some water!

The blast must've ripped someone's arm right off...

Even with everything burned around here, you can still get water!

This should do it.

Wha-?!

Water. Water.

That man's just letting his loincloth drag along the ground. How disgusting!

T-that's not a loincloth. It's the skin from his back...!

Groan...

Oh no!

Water. Water.

That man is dragging something, too.

89

90

SPLASH!

You idiot, Natsue! They're just burns! You don't have to die because your face is burnt!

Some-body, help us!

Hey, those kids are drowning!

Here, grab hold of this!

Gasp...

Pant pant...

Cough cough...

You can't give up, Natsue! Please don't die!

Sob...

No! I wanna die! Don't try to stop me!

.....

PUTT-PUTT-PUTT-PUTT

The boat's here. Everybody get on board!

PUTT-PUTT-PUTT

Hurry up now!

Aghh...

Ah...

TROMP TROMP TROMP

We're going to Ninoshima Island, Natsue. We'll get your burns treated there. So hang on.

Moan...

 In you go.

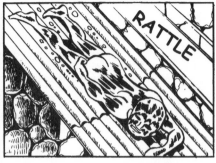 RATTLE

 KATHUNK

 This work is endless. The bodies just keep coming...

 Oof.

 RRRIP

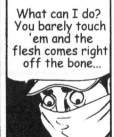 What can I do? You barely touch 'em and the flesh comes right off the bone...

94

RATTLE

They're loading them like so many sacks of potatoes! But just a while ago they were living people, laughing and crying...

We can't fit any more.

OK, let's head for Ninoshima.

PUTT-PUTT

PUTT-PUTT

It's too much, it's just too much...

PUTT-PUTT

PUTT-PUTT

95

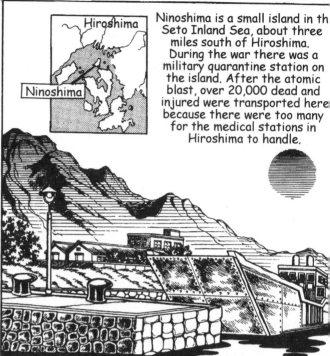

Ninoshima is a small island in th Seto Inland Sea, about three miles south of Hiroshima. During the war there was a military quarantine station on the island. After the atomic blast, over 20,000 dead and injured were transported here because there were too many for the medical stations in Hiroshima to handle.

Hiroshima

Ninoshima

Soldier, please help me.

Please, give me water...

Help me...

Mommy, Mommy...

Groan...

Medic, this man's dead. Get him out of here.

Yes sir.

96

..... Geez! They keep dying so fast, we don't get a moment's rest!

There's so many wounded people, they can't fit 'em all in this building... Why'd we even bother to come here?

I just wish they'd hurry up and treat you...

Gen, please, bring me some water...

Water? Again?

Please... Hurry...

Well, all right -- but if I leave you alone, how do I know you won't try to kill yourself?

I-I won't do that.

Are you sure? Because if you do, I'll be real mad at you!

You promise, Natsue?

I-I promise...

All right. I'll go get some water for you. Wait here.

.....

I-I'm sorry, Gen.

I'll never forget your kindness to me... never.

Puff puff... Natsue, I've brought you some water.

Oh!

S-she's gone. Where is she?

She headed toward the sea.

Oh no! She lied to me after all...!

Natsue! Natsue!!

Where are you, Natsue?

98

Gasp

Huff

Puff

Oh, no!

I was afraid of this!

STOP!!

Ah!

You promised you wouldn't try to kill yourself!

Please, let me die! I don't want to live with a face like this....

You fool! You fool!

99

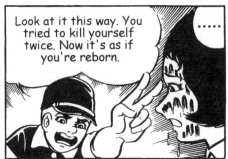

You'll never ever try to kill yourself again?

N-no. I promise.

I was thinking only about myself. But I know lots of people are dying no matter how much they want to live. I should be thankful I'm alive.

That's the spirit, Natsue! Hang in there!

T-thank you, Gen.

Gen, do you know the Cherry Blossom Song?

Uh, sort of...

If you sing it for me, I'll dance!

Ready?

Ulp! I'm not very good...

From somewhere afar ♪

Sweetly wafts the fragrance ♪

March sky is veiled in a spring haze... ♪

of the cherry blossoms... ♪

101

102

Sob... Today is the last day of my dream of becoming a dancer... I'll never dance again...

This must be so hard for her... If it weren't for her burns, she could've been a famous dancer!

Sob...

I-I know it's tough, Natsue, but you'll make it, I know you will!

Yes, yes I will. I'll survive somehow, no matter what happens...

Natsue...

T... thanks, Gen!

Hurry. Let's get them to take care of your burns.

Y... yeah.

Natsue found the will to live -- but was she really better off surviving?

The keloid scars from the burns stayed with her for the rest of her life. Natsue's life would be a hard one...

People are dying faster than we can burn 'em!

Man, I'm beat...

CLUNK CLANG

What're they digging over there?

There's not enough time to cremate all the bodies, so they're burying 'em in a mass grave.

All right, cover 'em up.

Yes, sir.

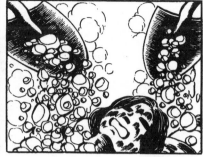

.....

.....

Don't become one of them, Natsue. You've got to survive!

Y-yeah.

I have to go back to Hiroshima now.

My mother's waiting. If I don't bring her some rice soon, my baby sister will die.

.....

Hang in there, OK, Natsue? Don't give up!

I-I won't...

See you in Hiroshima when you get better!

Y-yeah.

105

Gen... You take care of yourself, too. I'll never forget your kindness. Never...

.....

Good-bye...

Good-bye, Natsue.

Goodbye triangle, square like tofu! Tofu is white, white like a rabbit! A rabbit hops, hops like a frog! A frog is green...

.....

Puff puff...

Gotta hurry, find some rice...

Go on, kid, get outta here!!

.....

C'mon, mister, can't you spare just a little rice to help my baby sister...?

Forget it! We don't have enough to feed ourselves! Why would I give any rice to a complete stranger?!

Now scram! Shoo! Go away!

.....

P-please, sir. I'll do anything if you give me some rice. Even just a little -- please!

I told you already -- No!! Now leave, or I'll ladle this raw manure right on YOU!

What a cold-hearted old geezer! He won't even help a baby whose life is in danger!

Scram, I said!!

You stingy old stinker!

All you cripples from Hiroshima are nothing but trouble. Coming to our island, trampling our fields...

Please, ma'am. Please give me some rice...

Didn't you hear me? No. We don't have any rice. Get out of here.

Go, or I'll call the police!

.....

It's no use...

You've got a lot of nerve, sonny, asking for free handouts of rice!

What makes you think we have any to spare? Go on, get out!

Sniff... Nobody will give me any rice...

What'll I do? What'll I do?!

Mama, tell me. What should I do?...

WAH! WAH! WAH!

Dammit! My sister must be starving by now!

Somebody left a good sickle here...

Help! A thief!

All right, mister! Hand over your rice!

Those bastards! If they won't give me any rice, I'll do whatever I have to... rob, steal, even kill...!

Order in the court!

All right, Taro, you murdered someone, so I sentence you to death by hara-kiri!

Death by hara-kiri, Your Honor?

That's right. Hurry up!

Yes, sir.

Aha!

HEH HEH

Who are you?

Er, ahem!

Don't you guys want to see a REAL hara-kiri?

Huh! Someone's really doing it? Where?

You wanna see?

Yeah!

Yeah! Me too.

OK. I'll show you a real hara-kiri, but first everyone has to bring some rice here.

Rice?

Those who don't bring any rice can't watch.

So who's gonna do the hara-kiri?

Me!

I'll cut my own belly.

Y...you sure? You'll really cut it?

Yep, with this sickle. Just watch!

He's crazy, isn't he?

Who cares, if he really does it!

Yeah, I wanna see this.

OK, we'll bring some rice, but you better really do it!

Don't worry. Just bring plenty of rice!

Wait right there! We'll be back with the rice!

Hey, don't forget to bring a bag, too.

We got it!!

Yahoo!!

Hee hee... Here they come!

111

Here, we brought you the rice!

Hurry up and do the hara-kiri!

No need to rush.

Wow, this must be a good four kilos of rice!

OK, I shall now proceed to cut open my belly, so watch carefully...

Gulp.

Whoa! Not so close. When I cut myself, the blood's gonna spurt out. You don't want it all over your clothes!

Step back a ways!

Is this far enough?

No. No.

Get waaay back!

Is this OK?

No, farther!

112

Hey, he's running away!

I'm outta here!

SCOOT

Hey, he tricked us!

Wait up!

Stop! Rice thief!!

Sorry, boys, but I need this rice for my baby sister!

Stop, thief!

Catch him!

Don't let him get away!

Huff puff...

Ack!

SPLASH!

113

Agghh! What a stink!!

Hey he fell into a cess-pool!

Serves him right!

Help!!

Try and cheat us, will you?!

Take that!

Hit him!

Oww!

Sob... It's no use, I can never get away with anything!

Grab the rice.

Right!

Wait! Let me have it... Please!

Shut up! If you try to cheat us again, you'll be sorry!

114

..... Haw haw! Stew in that juice for a while, shithead!

Yahh! Serves you right!

Sob... Rice... I need rice...

Waah! I need rice...

Somebody, anybody, give me some rice. Help my little sister...

Please... Someone help her...

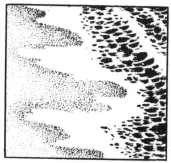

Sob... Sniff...

 What'll I do? I didn't know people could be so mean... If it weren't for that damn bomb, I wouldn't be in this fix...

 "SOB SNIFFLE SOB"

 I-I can't waste my time crying like this. I've got to find some rice!

 I'll try and ask someone again...

 This body must've floated all the way here from Hiroshima... And the crabs are eating what's left of it!

 Scram, you parasites! Leave him alone!

 Stupid crabs...

Ha ha ha!

Ho ho!

Gab gab

Blab blab

.....

Look at them, having a nice dinner together... They're so lucky...

Hey Daddy! Let's play sumo!

Sure, son, I'll take you on!

Beat him, bro!

I'll get you, Daddy!

Yay! Beat him, Gen!

I'll get you, Papa!

HEY-HO! PLINKETY PLINK!

There was a wife who loved her husband, and he adored his wife...

HA HA HA HA!

HA HA HA!

What a happy family... We were like that too, just a while ago...

HEE HEE HEE!

But now... just because we lived in Hiroshima... my family's gone...

Sob...

Moan...

Hey, who's there?!

118

Er, heh heh... Good evening, sir...

What do you want?

Do you like old folk ballads?

Sure, I like 'em a lot. Why?

Well, I'll sing one for you if you give me some rice.

You? Sing a ballad?!

Yessir, I'm pretty good, so please give me a chance...

Fair enough. If you're no good, I won't give you a thing.

But if you're really good, you'll get your rice!

R-really, sir? You promise?

What are you saying, dear? We can't spare any rice!

Relax. We'll just listen to him and tell him he's no good.

That way we get a little free entertainment!

Oooh, you're too clever, dear!

Go ahead, sonny!

I will now sing "The Miracle of Tsubosaka"...

AHEM!

119

There was a wife who loved her husband, and he adored his wife...

Hey-ho!

Now one fine day in the middle of June...

Hey-ho!

It was hot way out in the country-side.

Hey-ho! Plinkety-plink!

But cool deep in the woods...

Walk more slowly, Sawaichi, you know you can't see well!

OK, OK!

Shinji... Shinji...

120

....

Hey-ho,
hey-ho...!

Remembering the happy days
when he performed the same
song with Shinji, Gen sang with
all his heart. His voice rose
and fell like the tide, moving
the hearts of all who listened...

T-that's
all... I'm
done...

....

G-go bring
him some
rice...

Y-yes,
dear...
Sniffle...

A promise
is a promise.
Here's your
rice!

THUD!

R-really,
sir?
You'll
let me
take it?!

121

Rice... I finally got some rice...

T-thank you, sir! Thank you, ma'am!

Come back and sing for us again. Next time we'll get the whole village to come listen.

Hey, you're pretty good! I was surprised!

Yeah, me too!

......

Look Mama, I finally got some rice!

Just wait a little longer. I'll be back soon!

Hurrah! Hurrah!

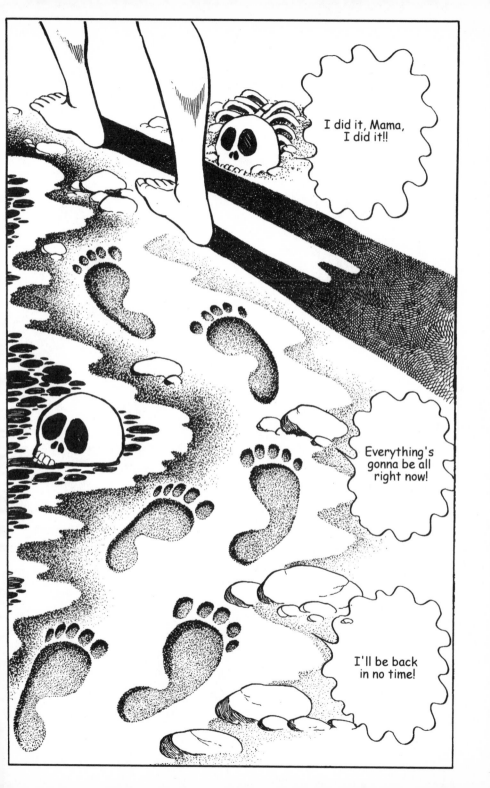

125

I hear a new-fangled bomb was dropped on Hiroshima, boy... They say nothing will grow there for the next sixty years.

Sixty years!?

It's horrible... Hiroshima's been turned into a graveyard.

W-what will happen to my family? I'm scared...

I have to find my sister in Hiroshima. She married a man there. I'm worried about her. I hope she's alive...

Look!

That's Hiroshima!

What's that smoke?

They're burning bodies.

Hard to believe... The only thing moving there is the smoke from burning bodies.

Just three days ago, it was such a lively town...

Look, Mama! I've brought you some rice!

PUTT-PUTT-PUTT

PUTT-PUTT   PUTT-PUTT

Thanks, mister!

Sure.

Gotta hurry.

I can't wait to see Mama. Boy, will she be glad!

Oh, when I get older
I wanna be a soldier
With a sword and a horse
And lots of medals of course
Hup! Hup! Giddy-up!

.....

BAM BAM

Daisuke, Jiro, Yukiko: Father and Mother are with relatives in Kabe. Come quickly.

Let's go, dear. Cheer up -- if our kids are alive they'll see this sign and come looking for us...

It's no use waiting for them here. We've already looked all over for them...

Sob...

128

Genkichi, Miyo: Come to Gion-cho.

Eizo and Hanayo: We are in Eba.

Taro, Kunio, Akiko, Yasuko: Mother is with our relatives in Itsukaichi.

Hmm... Everyone's putting up signs to tell their families where they are...

I should put one up, too.

My brothers might come looking for us...

Koji, Akira, hurry up and come back!

I wish they were here... I'm lonely...

Wha-?!

129

SMASH

BAM BAM

CRACK

What's that lady doing? Looks like she's smashing a skull...

BAM BAM BAM BAM

What a weird thing to do!

Groan...

This'll make you feel better soon, Kozo, so be patient...

SPRINKLE

130

Now swallow this...

COUGH COUGH

T-that's awful -- she's feeding him powdered bones!

Uh, Ma'am, how come you're giving him powdered bones? Is that really good for him...?

Mind your own business, boy!

Putting human bone powder on burns makes them heal.

And if you swallow it, it'll keep you from dying.

No! that's not true. That's just a superstition!

Hush, boy! Lots of people have been saved this way!

Here, you should take some too. It'll keep you from getting sick.

Ugh! N-no thanks!

Well, suit yourself... I was just trying to help you...

Even if it is a superstition, I'll believe in it if it heals my son's burns!

131

SPRINKLE

That woman's doing the same thing.

People sure come up with some weird ideas...

They'll believe anything if they think it will save their loved ones...

I wonder who started this story about the powdered bones...?

ROAR

It's a B-29!

It's flying low, so the war must still be going on.

ROAR

You idiots! What are you here for?

There's nothing left in Hiroshima for you to bomb!

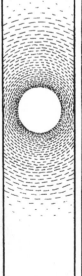

I'm back, Mama! Here, I brought you some rice!

G... Gen!

Gen! You had me so worried! You've been gone two whole days...

.....

M- Mama!

Sob... It was so hard, Mama... It was so hard to find any rice...

Gen...

T-thank you, Gen. Thank you for the rice...

G... Gen!

W-what happened to your hair? You're bald!

Sniff... I don't know. It just fell out all of a sudden...

Y-you aren't suffering from pain or anything, are you, Gen?

N-no... I feel fine, Mama...

Are you sure, Gen? Don't lie to me now!

I'm fine, Mama. Really!

Oh Gen! Please, please don't die. If I lost you too, I'd go mad...

I won't die, Mama! I promise!

135

But I wonder why you lost all your hair...

Luckily, I got a hold of some good medicine!

Take this. It'll keep you from getting sick.

Here you go.

OK, Mama...

Gulp.

Yuck! This tastes terrible!

N-no! It can't be...?!

M-Mama... That wasn't bone powder, was it?

Why, yes. How did you know?

Gag!!

Barf... Gasp... How could YOU believe that stupid superstition, too?!

I'll believe anything if it keeps you from getting sick...

Perfectly healthy people are suddenly losing their hair, getting diarrhea and dying! So I'm worried about you!

I've got to believe in something, even a silly super-stition!

.....

I-I'm sorry, Mama... I didn't know how you felt...

Phew! It sure tasted awful, though!

How's the baby, Mama?

She's OK. A very kind woman has been nursing her for me...

GOO GOO

Hey, Sis! I was worried about you!

GAH GOO

Hee hee... I'm so glad you're OK!

GOO GOO

You must be hungry, Gen. I'll cook some of this rice for you.

Oh boy!

Where did you get all these pots and pans, Mama?

I found them here and there in the ruins...

Eat your fill, Gen. We only have salt to put on it, though...

YOU eat lots, too, Mama, so you can nurse the baby!

Wow! A whole bowl of pure rice!!

I feel like I'm dreaming...

MUNCH

Mmm! It tastes so good I can't stand it!!

I'll eat it one grain at a time to make it last...

Gee, Mama, I wish Eiko and Shinji were here to eat this, too...

I-I know...

138

WAAH! Mama! Gen stole one of my grains of rice!

If I could eat a whole bowl of rice, I could die happy!

.....

Sob...

Gasp!

No!!

It can't be!

139

SHINJI!!

S-Shinji!
You're alive?!
But...

Heh
heh.

GRAB!

Shinji,
wait!

Shinji,
where are
you
going?!

I-I must be dreaming...
B-but that IS Shinji...

Hurry, Gen! Bring him back!

He must have run off with our rice as a joke!

Wait, Shinji!

Yahoo! He's alive!

I can't believe it! He's alive!

Hey, Shinji! Stop!

Pant Pant...

.....

He must be hiding in this air raid shelter!

Hey, Shinji, come on out!

Where are you, Shinji?

We'll play hide and seek tomorrow. Stop kidding and come out.

BONK!

WHACK!

WHAM!

Oww...

THUD

DRIP DRIP

Is he out?

Yeah, I think so.

Let's have some light!

FLASH

142

What a pest! He followed me all the way here!

All right, men! I've got some food for you. A whole bag of rice!

Yee-haw!

What are we going to do with him?

Hah! Just bury him somewhere!

143

144

145

Kaff kaff... At ease, men!

I am happy to report the procurement of this fine bag of rice today...

This should keep us going for a while.

Thank you for your great efforts, Food Commander.

We are grateful as always, sir, heh heh!

We never cease to be impressed by your food procurement abilities, Commander! Ha ha!

Hmph.

Once again, let us pay our respects...

To Food Commander Ryuta! Ten-SHUN!!

Thankew, thankew!

Well, men, I expect you're all a little hungry.

Rations will now be distributed.

Hur-rah!

Hur-rah!

Dinner-time! Dinner-time!

Every-one line up!

BANG BANG

Is... is this ALL...?!

Don't complain, stupid! If we eat it all at once, what will we eat tomorrow?

Heh heh Guess you're right, Ryuta.

Make sure you chew it slowly,

so it'll expand in your stomachs.

Aye aye, sir!

MUNCH MUNCH

CRUNCH CRUNCH

Heh heh! Rice always tastes good.

MUNCH

Yeah!

147

Hey, you guys!

Acorn is back from his scouting mission!

Find any-thing, Acorn?

Sure did!!

Great news! They're going to be passing out rice balls soon!

Rice balls? Really?!

Banzai!

Yahoo! Rice balls! We can save this uncooked rice for later!

Carrot, take the basket!

Onion, you take the pot!

Aye aye!

Yessir!

All set?

Ready for battle, sir!

Vroomm! Vroomm!

Charge! Don't let 'em get away!

Yay!

TROMP TROMP

Yahoo!

PLINK

SPLOSH

Groan...

Huh? W- where am I?!

Now I remember... I chased Shinji in here and then something hit me!

Wha-?

Look what he did to the rice -- and after all the trouble I went through to get it...!

Where is that numb-skull?

Shinji! Shinji!

Where are you? Come out!

149

SCRAPE

Cheer up, ma'am! These should help a little.

Thank you, soldier!

PLOP

Give me lots, mister! There's seven in my family!

Ten in mine!!

Ten in mine, too!

Here you go, boys. Stay healthy!

SCRAPE

PLOP

Hee hee! Look at all these beautiful rice balls!

Yeah, I'm so happy I almost wet my pants!

151

152

S... Shinji!

Uh oh... He's come to!

We should've buried him right away!

Damn! He's mad as hell because I stole his rice! Battle positions, everyone!

Right!

Ha ha! I won't let you get away this time, Shinji!

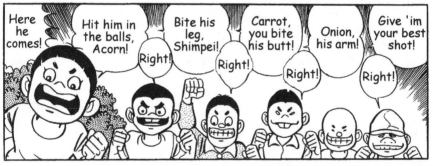

Here he comes!

Hit him in the balls, Acorn!

Right!

Bite his leg, Shimpei!

Right!

Carrot, you bite his butt!

Right!

Onion, his arm!

Give 'im your best shot!

Right!

Shinji!

Yikes!

Kamikaze crotch attack!!

You've got it all wrong, Shinji. Mama and I have been worried sick about you! C'mon, let's go home.

Shut up! Stop calling me "Shinji"!

I'm not Shinji!

I'm Ryuta. Ryuta Kondo.

And I don't have a brother like you!

No... That's not true.

You're Shinji! Admit it!

You're just kidding around with me, right?

Hee hee! I'm so glad you're alive, Shinji!

Ack! Stop! It tickles!!

You must be crazy! Go away!

You're the one who's crazy, Shinji! You must've forgotten everything because of the shock from the bomb and the fire!

Sob... Shinji, please, you've got to remember me...

GASP

Heh heh... Look at that -- he's crying!

CRY BABY!

Shinji, don't you remember all the things we did together? Begging, singing songs...?

Shut up! My family was just Mom, Dad and me.

I've never seen you before!

M...my mom and dad were...

T...they were...

156

What're you doing, Ryuta?

Shhh... Don't move! I'm going to catch this big cicada!

FLASH!

Oww!

Groan... P...Papa! Mama!

Papa! Mama! Jiro! Keiko!

My whole family was killed when our house collapsed...

Mine, too.

See, I'm not Shinji! So stop following me around!

.....

We survive by sticking together... so don't get in our way!

Let's go, men.

Sniffle

Sniff

Sob...

Hey, what's the matter?! C'mon, let's sing a song!

YEAH!

Left, right! Left, right! I left my wife with seventeen kids

160

Nothing in the cupboard
but old rice balls
Left, right! Left, right!

.....

N-no...

No!!

It's not true!

It's a lie!!

Waaah!
That's Shinji!
It's got to be!!

...So he wasn't Shinji after all... His name is Ryuta...?

They say everyone in the world has at least four doubles... That boy certainly looked just like Shinji...

I know it's hard to accept, Gen, but Shinji is dead... You've got to give up thinking he's alive...

No! No! I won't give up!!

162

He IS Shinji! I'll make him admit that he is!

Poor Gen. He really believes that boy is Shinji...

We can't stay here forever, Gen.

I know someone in Eba. Let's go there.

A relative?

No, she's a friend of mine.

All of your father's relatives and mine were in Hiroshima... They may all be dead...

Koji and Akira haven't come back yet. Let's put up a sign where the house was, and go to Eba.

浩二あんちゃん
昭あんちゃん
えと
おがあちゃんは
江波にいる

To Koji and Akira: Mother and Gen are in Ebd.

I'll go find some wood for the sign, Mama.

Thank you, Gen.

.....

BAM BAM
BAM BAM
BAM BAM

.....

BAM BAM
BAM BAM

Mr...
Mr.
Pak!

BAM BAM
BAM

Hur-
rah!
It's
Mr.
Pak!!

BAM BAM
BAM

Did you
find
your
father,
Mr.
Pak?

BAM BAM
BAM

Mr. Pak!
What're
you
making?

164

Mr. Pak...?

Gasp!

W-what a nasty look! What's the matter with him?!

BAM BAM BAM

Mr... Mr. Pak?

No! Get away from me!

Ack!

165

W-what's the matter, Mr. Pak?

I hate them... I hate the Japanese!

Why are you so angry, Mr. Pak? Did you find your father?

Yes, I found him...

W-was he dead...?

He was killed.

K... killed?

My father was killed because he was Korean!

W-why? What happened?

.....

F-Father... You survived the blast! Thank heaven!

Aigo... Aigo...

I can't stand it any longer...

Hold on, Father. I'll take you to the medical station.

Groan...

Don't give up, Father... Please don't die!

Moan...

Agh...

Please, Doctor... Please examine my father...

Aigo...

Aigo...

A Korean, eh?

We've been waiting over five hours. Please help him...

I don't have time to treat Koreans. You'll have to wait!

W... what?!

Doctor, we were forced to come to Japan. Yet we've fought right alongside you in this war. We've worked as hard as you for this country! Why won't you treat my father?!

Shut up!

167

We treat our own first. Koreans come later. We don't have enough medicine anyway. Stop complaining!

·····

Y-you'd even discriminate against the wounded and dying...?!

Moan...

A-are you in pain, Father? Hold on, hold on...

Damn them, we'll go to another medical station...

Please, Doctor, help my father...

A Korean...?

Sign: Medical Station Mortality List

168

Please, sir, he needs treatment now!

All right. All right. Later.

I'm too busy to treat any Koreans right now...

.....

Bastards! It's the same here, too!

GASP! AAGHH!

F-Father!

Father!!

Even if he was beyond help, they should have treated him like a human being! I only wanted him to die with some dignity!

.....

How low do the Japanese have to make us feel...?!

And that's not all. They just leave the bodies of dead Koreans where they are, like so much garbage...

The Japanese don't think of us as human. I'll never forget the way they've treated us...

.....

At least I can give my father a decent coffin to be cremated in...

I-is that his coffin you're building?

.....

BAM BAM BAM

SAW SAW

SAW SAW

I'm sorry, Gen -- I shouldn't have yelled at you like that. You've done nothing wrong.

It's OK, Mr. Pak. You have a right to be angry.

When I grow up, Mr. Pak, I won't treat Koreans like that, I promise!

Hang in there, Mr. Pak!

T-thanks, Gen...

BAM BAM

SAW SAW

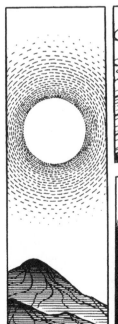

Have a safe journey home, Father, and rest in peace...

171

CRACKLE
CRACKLE

CREAAKKK

CREAAKKK

BANG!

Ack!

The coffin burst open from the heat...!

Oh no!!

H-his body is rearing up -- just like a fish on a grill...!

So you're still not ready to leave this world, Father? I understand... You were looking forward so much to the day you could return to Korea...

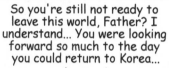

ROAR

Sob...

.....

Look, Ryuta, it's him!

What's he doing with that Korean? Let's have a little fun with him...

173

174

I don't ever want to hear you make fun of Koreans!

The government tries to get us to fight their wars by telling us the Koreans and Chinese are weak and stupid. Don't be fooled by their lies! You should respect everyone, no matter where they come from!

So what are you making fun of Koreans for, Shinji?!

Don't ever do it again, you hear me?!

OW-OW-OW!!

I'm not Shinji, I'm Ryuta! Cut it out already!!

Urk!

I'll get even with you yet!

YAAH! STUPID BALDY! BED-WETTER!

W-wasn't that Shinji? Is he still alive?!

He says he's not Shinji -- but I know he is!

175

H-he looks just like Shinji! I can't believe it... I was sure he died in the fire...

My husband... my children...!

It's no use, Ma'am!!

Have you dug up the bones of your family, Gen?

.....

You should dig them up as soon as you can. They must be crying to be taken out from under the rubble...

Stop it, Mr. Pak! Shinji, Eiko and Papa are still alive!

They're alive!!

G... Gen...

I don't like you, Mr. Pak!

Gen... I shouldn't have said that to you...

Everybody wants to believe his family is alive...

Let's both be strong, Gen. Let's not give up...

I'll become stronger... Just watch...

.....

177

Pant
pant...

Mr...Mr.
Pak was
right...

I've got to
go look for
their bones.

If I find their
bones, I'll know
for sure if
Shinji's dead
or alive.

I'll go to where
our house was
and dig them
up now!

Up you go!

Weren't we lucky to find this abandoned cart...

Well, I've loaded all our belongings...

We're ready to go to Eba now...

.....

Gen, have you put up the sign for Koji and Akira?

We have to tell them that we're going to stay with the Hayashis in Eba.

No, not yet.

Go put it up, so we can leave right away.

Yes, Mama...

Gen... What are you going to do with the bucket?

I'm going to get the bones...

Bones...?

Whose bones...?!

179

Papa, Eiko and Shinji's bones, of course!

W-what!

Stop, Gen!

T-there aren't any bones! Everyone's still alive!

Isn't that right, Gen?

What's the matter, Mama? You're the one who said I should give up hoping they're alive.

I...I can't face it.

I don't want to see their bones...

To know they're really dead... To lose all hope of ever seeing them again... I-I'm afraid...

M... Mama...

Gen... Let's not do it now.

No, Mama! I have to! If their bones really are buried there, they must be crying to be dug up!

I can't leave them like that...

I'll dig them up now.

P...please don't do it, Gen.

I have to know whether that boy Ryuta is really Shinji or not. I don't want to keep hanging on to false hopes!

G... Gen...

.....

This is where my house was...

Papa's paint boxes are all warped from the heat...

T-this is where they were trapped under the house...

Here... under this rubble...

.....

H-help me, Gen! I'm burning! Help me!!

I-it hurts...

Hurry, Gen! Take your mother and run, before you get caught in the fire!

184

SHIVER

T-they're here...

This m-must be Shinji...

.....

DAMN! DAMN! DAMN!

Dammit!

186

NO!

T-this big one is Papa...

And this... is Eiko...

Wow! Look at all the locusts, Gen!

Gen, let's race to the field!

Be strong, Gen, no matter how many times you're stepped on. Just like wheat!

Sob...

T-they're really dead... Shinji... Eiko... Papa...

They're not alive anymore...

You've changed... you've all changed...

浩二あんちゃん
昭あんちゃん
元とおかあちゃん
は江波の林さんの家に

To Koji and Akira: Mother and Gen are at the Hayashis in Eba.

SCRAPE

RATTLE

188

RATTLE

....

Hey, you! You had some nerve hitting me like that! Now you're gonna pay for it!

.....

.....

Hey, wait! You chicken or some-thing?!

Get him, boys! Don't let him run away!

YEAH! YEAH!

Here! This is what you get for hitting Ryuta!

BONK!

189

Yeah! This'll teach you to mess with our Food Commander!

Grrr!! CHOMP!

Take that! BONK!

..... Hey! What's the matter? C'mon and fight!

Idiot! Baldy! Don't ever talk big to me again! You hear?!

.....

WOBBLE

CLATTER

Jeez, what a wimp!

Maybe he's just dumb.

Can't he feel anything?

Hmph. That's weird -- first he keeps calling me Shinji, and now he won't even look at me...

What a creep.

190

All...all our hopes are gone now, Gen...

We know... they're really dead...

.....

But... we had to know the truth sooner or later...

There's nothing we can do. We'll just have to pick ourselves up and head for Eba...

I forgot something down here, Gen. I'll go get it...

.....

I wonder what's taking Mama so long...?

Ah!

Sob... Sob... Sob...

Sob... Sob... Sob...

M... Mama...

Oh, my dear husband... I want to die, too!

I don't want to go on living. I don't care any longer...

N-no!

WAAAH!!

I'm sorry, Mama! I shouldn't have dug up their bones! Please don't die, Mama!

G... Gen...

SOB WAIL SOB

Oh, Gen!

Mama! Mama!

193

Sob...
Sob...

Sob...
Sniff...

I...I won't die, Gen. How could I leave my children alone? I haven't forgotten what your father told me...

You've got to survive, Kimie! For the sake of the child you're carrying -- and for Gen, and for Koji and Akira when they return! You've got to be there for them!

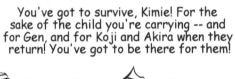

Sniff...

I'm sorry, Gen. I just felt so over-whelmed...

Let's go to Eba.

It will do us good to go somewhere far from these bad memories!

We'll be all right, Gen. Cheer up, now!

Y-yeah, you too, Mama...

194

Are you OK, Gen?

Nothing to it, Mama!

HEAVE-HO! HEAVE-HO!

We'll have to start all over in Eba. I must be strong...

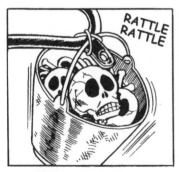

RATTLE RATTLE

Papa, Eiko, Shinji... From now on we'll always be together. I'll take you to Eba with us!

Don't worry about us! We'll be fine!

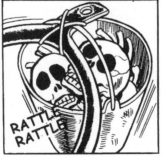

RATTLE RATTLE

The bones are rattling in the bucket. It sounds like they're crying...

195

So that's why he didn't say anything... He dug up Shinji's bones...

I guess we shouldn't have been so mean to him...

Y... yeah...

But he's lucky. At least he still has his mother...

Wow, Mama! Eba sure has a lot of boats!

That's right. It's a fishing village.

How much farther to Mrs. Hayashi's house?

We're almost there...

How did you and Mrs. Hayashi become friends?

We grew up in the same neighborhood, so we played and went to school together.

Look, Gen. See that mountain with the weather station on top? Her house is at the foot of it.

197

People around here are lucky. The bomb only broke their windows and tilted the houses a bit.

Yes. The fires didn't reach here...

Why, it's Kimie!

Kimie Nakaoka!

Y-you're safe! I'm so glad!

Kiyo...!

I've been so worried about you. It's awful what happened in Hiroshima...

Kiyo, I'm sorry to have to ask this, but could you put us up here for a while?

For heaven's sake, don't apologize! You can stay as long as you like!

T- thank you, Kiyo!

Gen, this is Kiyo.

Hi, nice to meet you, Ma'am!

Hello, Gen.

Kimie, where are your husband and the other children?

.....

.....

Oh, Kimie...

.....

It...it must have been terrible, Kimie. But I know you'll survive...

T-thank you, Kiyo...

Well, we can talk later... Come on in and get some rest now.

199

This is my mother-in-law...and my children, Tatsuo and Takeko.

Mother, this is my dear friend Kimie. Please let her stay with us for a while.

.....

I'm sorry to impose on you like this...

WHACK!

Kiyo! This is a house, not a hotel!

M-Mother...

We must take good care of this house until my son comes back from the war.

It wouldn't do to let some stranger come into his house and dirty it, now would it?!

200

But Mother, my friend is in trouble. She needs our help.

Hmph. Fine, go ahead, suit yourself.

....

Don't let Mother upset you, Kimie. She's just a little cranky.

I'm sorry to trouble you so, Kiyo.

Tatsuo, Takeko, this is your new friend, Gen. Be nice to him, all right?

Uh, sure.

Hey, didja bring us any gifts?

Gifts...?

Yeah! You're supposed to bring a gift when you stay in someone's house!

Don't talk such nonsense! Gen's house burned down and they have nothing left!

Huh! No gifts? What kind of dumb kid is he?!

.....

I'm...I'm sorry about that, Kimie. I'll talk to them later. Please don't pay them any mind.

201

 Well, you must be hungry. I'll go fix dinner, so why don't you get a little rest.

Thank you, Kiyo.

 .....

Mama... They don't like us, do they.

I know, Gen.

But we have nowhere to go. We have no choice but to stay here for a while.

We'll repay them for their kindness later, somehow.

Gen, how long has it been since we last sat on nice tatami mats?

I love the smell of tatami!

It's like a dream...

Hmph!

202

Sign: Prevent Fires

It's not much, but please go ahead and eat.

Thank you.

Gen, say thank you before you start!

Gulp! Thank you! Oh boy!

What's going on, Mom? I don't have as much rice as usual!

Me either!

Everybody has the same amount, so don't complain. I'll steam some potatoes for you later.

No! I want more rice!!

We don't have much rice! You know that!

More! More!

203

You gave our rice to them! THAT'S why we have less!!

Give me back my rice!

.....

.....

Hush your mouth! You should know better at your age!

Waahh! She hit me!

You didn't have to hit him, Kiyo. He's only saying what's true.

Here, Kiyo. Give this to Tatsuo. I don't need it.

I...I'm sorry, Kimie...

My children are very spoiled. Please, just ignore them and go ahead and eat.

No, it's our fault for imposing on you...

That girl gives me the creeps, staring at my rice like that...

Huh! I'd better eat it fast.

Thank you, Ma'am!

BWAAH!

W...what's wrong, Takeko?

Wah! He ate my rice!

That's enough, Takeko!

Boo hoo hoo.

.....

.....

.....

.....

.....

Mama, I don't want to stay here.

Be patient, Gen. This isn't easy for them, either...

No matter what happens, you must behave yourself. Promise me, Gen?

Y-yes, Mama...

205

WAH! WAH!

There, there... Are you hungry?

WAH! WAH!

Here you are...

SLURP

I'm sorry, but your mother has no milk. You'll have to be content with this rice broth...

Hey Mama, let's choose a name for her!

We should, shouldn't we. What would be a good name?

I want her to have a name that will bring her love and happiness...

So, you mean you want her to have lots of friends?

Hmm...

How about Tomoko, Mama? Tomo means friend, so that should bring her lots of friends!

Tomoko...

That's a fine name, Gen. Let's call her Tomoko.

Yeah!

206

Grow up soon so you can help your mother, Tomoko!

GOO GOO

Heh heh! From today you're Tomoko Nakaoka!

I'm the one who named you. Good name, huh? How do you like it?

Grow up quick so we can play together, Tomoko!

Whoopee-do!

Gen, be careful...

I have to go wash her diapers now...

YAHOO!

Look at them, acting like this is their own house.

They make me mad!

And as long as they stay here, they're gonna keep eating our rice, Takeko.

Yeah. I don't like that.

We've got to get rid of them somehow...

That's right, throw 'em out!

Grand-ma...

207

I don't care if she's Kiyo's best friend, this is no time to worry about others! We don't even have enough food for ourselves. We should kick 'em out!

Tatsuo, Takeko, you have my permission to make life so miserable for them, they have no choice but to move out!

Y-yes Ma'am!

Leave it to us, Grandma!

Heh heh.

Hey you!

What?

BIFF!

Take your hat off when you're in our house!

.....

Hey look, Takeko! He's bald! Haw haw!

Tee hee! Look at that! He's really, really bald!

One! He's bald, he's bald on top! Two! He's bald, his head will rot! Three! He's bald, as bald can be! Four! He's bald, for all to see!

Five! He's bald, his head's all skin! Six! He's bald, his hair grows in!

Seven! He's bald, just look, you'll know! Eight! He's bald, his head shines so! Nine! He's bald, his head got fried! Ten! He's bald, on every side!

WHAP WHAP WHAP

HAW HAW! HEE HEE!

What's this baby's name?

T... Tomoko.

Let me hold her.

N-no! You can't, she was just born!

Hmph! Stingy stinker! Well, I don't care. She's got a face like a monkey!

.....

Why, that little... How dare she call Tomoko a...

Nyah! Nyah! Monkey face! Monkey face!

.....

WAAH!

WAH! WAH!
Uh oh, she's crying!

Hey you, what did you do to her?!
WAH WAH WAH WAH
No-thing.

Wha-!

You little rat. You pinched her!

Look, Tatsuo! Baldy's getting mad! His whole head is turning red as a beet!
Haw haw! Look at that! Go ahead, get madder, Baldy!

Why, you-!

Urk!
POW!
I'll show you!

210

You nasty brat! Hit my precious grand-children, will you?

Get down on your knees and apologize! No! They're the ones who were bad!

How dare you talk back to me, you little troublemaker!

Say you're sorry! WHACK! Ow!

Grrr...

Don't look at me like that! Say you're sorry! Now! WHACK!

Gen! What hap-pened? Moan...

You've done a poor job raising that child. He hit my grandchildren and won't even say he's sorry. I can't have a brat like him in this house. You'll have to leave!

Gen, hurry up and apologize! N... No!

It wasn't my fault. They pinched Tomoko and made fun of me...

Never mind! Just say you're sorry!

Why do I have to say I'm sorry, Mama?!

I didn't do anything wrong!

SLAP

I don't care! Say you're sorry!

N-No!

SLAP

Say you're sorry!

Say you're sorry! Now!

SLAP! SLAP!

Gen, you promised me, didn't you? That you'd behave, no matter what...

Oww...

Please forgive him. Please.

Shut up! I won't forgive him till he apologizes himself!

I'm so sorry for what he's done. Please accept my apology.

I don't want YOUR apology!

.....

Gen, please! Don't make it any harder for me...

All...all right. I'll apologize, Mama...

I'm...I'm sorry. I was wrong. Please forgive me...

Good. You should have said that at the beginning.

Don't you ever hit Tatsuo or Takeko again, or I'll throw you out. Hear me?

Ya hear her, Baldy?

Yaah! Baldy Baldy Baldy!!

.....

SOB

Sob... Sob...

Gen... You were very strong... Thank you...

I know it wasn't your fault, Gen. I know that.

214

If our home hadn't been destroyed by the bomb, you wouldn't have to go through this... It's hard to have to depend on the kindness of strangers...

.....

Good work, children. Keep giving them a hard time so they'll leave soon!

T-that hurt, Grandma...

If it hurt, then you should pay him back for it!

Y-yeah.

Once again, Gen learned how cruel the world can be and how hard it is to survive...

Takeko! Let me know if someone comes!

Right!

I got the rice. Let's go!

Good!

Hurry up and give me some! Hee hee!

Hey, take it easy!

Don't ever let Mom or Grandma find out about this, OK?

We'll be in real trouble if they find out we're stealing rice.

I know!

Sure tastes good, huh, Takeko.

CRUNCH CRUNCH

CRUNCH CRUNCH

Yeah.

Boy, do I hate that kid Gen and his family. Ever since they came, we don't get as much rice.

Yeah. They really get on my nerves.

Waahh! Waahh!

You're hungry, aren't you, Tomoko? Just a minute. I'll make you some more rice broth.

WAH! WAH!

Hey now, Tomoko! Don't cry!

There isn't much left of the rice Gen brought from Ninoshima. If I'm not careful, I'll have nothing to feed her...

217

..... Gen, look after Tomoko for a bit, will you?

Sure!

Hmph! The nerve, eating our precious rice while they keep their own hidden away!

What a sneak that woman is...

And where did they get that rice, anyway? I wonder...

.....

Grumble... Grumble...

That's odd...

What's wrong, Kiyo?

Some of our rice is gone. I wonder who took it.

W... what?!

I know!

Kiyo, you've let a terrible thief into our house.

Are...are you saying ...Kimie stole it...?

218

I just saw her! I saw Kimie with some rice she'd hidden away!

Kiyo, I want to make some rice broth for Tomoko. Can I use the stove?

S-sure, Kimie...

I won't let her get away with this.

T...there must be some mistake, Mother.

She DOES have rice...

Did you see that, Kiyo? How could she have rice if her house burned down? She must have stolen it.

.....

I can't have a thief like that in my house. I'm going to throw her out!

.....

Kimie, where did you get that rice?

This? Gen got it in Ninoshima and brought it back for Tomoko...

I know I should've given it to you... but I need it to feed Tomoko. Please forgive me.

I'll work to repay you for all you've given us, I promise. Please, just give me a little time...

You've got a lot of nerve talking like that, you thief!

T... thief?

You've been stealing our rice, haven't you! Admit it!

W...what are you saying?!

This...this isn't your rice. I'm not a thief.

It won't do you any good to deny it! I'm taking you to the police!

Come on, let's go!

K...Kiyo, I didn't steal your rice!

Please believe me, Kiyo!

.....

Ah!

WHACK

Shut up, you barefaced liar!

W-what are you doing?!

Mama...!

Urk!

Get away from her, you old hag!

How dare you hit my mother...

and call her a thief?!

I earned that rice myself. If you don't believe me, go to Ninoshima and ask!

Shut up, you brat! You're both shameless liars!

You old witch! Where's your proof that we stole anything?!

Some of our rice is missing! What more proof do I need?

Who else in this house would steal it?!

Let's go! We'll have the police look into this!

Don't go, Mama! You haven't taken anything!

It's all right, Gen. The police will investigate and find that I didn't do anything.

Huh! She's got some nerve...

Gen, give Tomoko her rice broth while I'm gone.

M-Mama...

Hurry up, now!

Heh heh... This is getting interesting!

Grandma's really giving 'em a hard time now!

D-damn them all...

I can't stand it, Tomoko, I can't stand it.

Yaah! Rice thief! Rice thief!

Y-you'll be sorry for this...

222

223

I haven't stolen any rice! Why do you assume that I did? Why don't you investigate?

Watch your tongue, woman!

I'm a busy man!

BANG

The citizens of Eba don't steal! We've had a lot of theft here only since you homeless beggars started pouring in from Hiroshima!

I haven't stolen anything.

Officer, put this woman in jail.

Grr...

What more do I have to say? Do you want to be locked up?!

I didn't do anything to be jailed.

Once I put you in jail, you won't get out for some time. You have a child and a baby, don't you? They're probably crying right now, waiting for you.

WAH! WAH! WAH!

224

Sob...

Here! Sign the apology!

G...Gen... I know it's wrong... but I must sign. I can't leave you and Tomoko alone...

So you finally admit to your crime, eh?

Ah...

Nakaoka

Kimie

Is this good enough, Mrs. Hayashi?

I'd rather see her in jail, but she's a close friend of my daughter in law's...

All right. You may go now, but don't ever steal rice again!

.....

Heh heh. Now they'll HAVE to leave!

Yaah! Thief!

Thief! Thief!

RUMBLE

Huff puff

.....

Ah!

226

Mama!

Pant pant... What are you doing here, Mama?

I've been looking all over for you!

W-why are you crying, Mama?

It's...it's nothing, Gen...

What's wrong?

The police proved you didn't steal the rice, didn't they?

......

Gen... That atomic bomb didn't just make it hell for the dying... but for the living too. If only that bomb hadn't fallen...

...your mother wouldn't have to endure this disgrace...

W-what happened?!

227

..... M-Mama! You didn't!!

How could you, Mama?! How could you let them call you a thief? We didn't steal their rice!

I had no choice. If I went to jail, what would become of you and Tomoko...?

Let's not go back to that house, Gen. Let's go somewhere else.

NO! We can't leave now! Not with them calling you a thief!

We've got to go back! We've got to prove to them you're not a thief! I'll find out who really stole the rice!

No, Gen, no! I can't bear to go back there...

Don't be a fool, Mama! You can't let them get away with that!

Come on, Mama! Let's go back! Don't give in to them!

Sob... Sob...

My mother's not a thief!

She's not!

Please, Mama, let's go back!

RUMBLE

Sleep, my baby, sleep... ♪

Of all the nerve! She comes right back here as if nothing happened!

Kiyo, go tell her they have to leave!

I-I can't say that to my friend...

Hmph! Well, if you can't, I will!

I want you to leave here at once. We can't have a thief staying in our house!

.....

When I've proved I'm not a thief, I'll leave. But I won't shame myself any further.

So you still insist you didn't steal anything, eh? You brazen creature!

You leave me no choice. I'll have the police come take you away.

.....

There's no one around, Tatsuo!

Good. Keep an eye out!

Heh heh. Once I start eating rice, I can't stop!

I got another bag full, Takeko. Let's go!

Goody!

THIEVES!

Thieves! Thieves! Everybody come quick!

CLANG! CLANG! CLANG!

Waah! I can't get up...!

Hah! I figured it was you two!

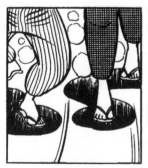

Urk!

Gasp!

Look, you old hag! These are your rice thieves!

Now you know we didn't do it!

Whimper...

Tatsuo! Takeko!

I'm...I'm sorry, M-Mom...

Old hag! Say you're sorry for calling my mother a thief!

Go to the police and tell them you were wrong!

Shut up! If you hadn't come to our house, this wouldn't have happened! You're the ones who should apologize!

Why, you... you ugly old witch...

Urk! W-what are you d-doing...

All you've done is give my mother a hard time... I'll show you!

GASP

Stop, Gen!

Let me go, Mama!

You proved that we're not thieves. That's enough, Gen.

Mrs. Hayashi is right. If we hadn't come here, this would never have happened. You mustn't blame her, Gen.

......

232

Now that you've proved I'm not a thief, I can leave this house with pride, Gen. Thank you.

Grr...

Goodbye, Kiyo. Please forgive us for causing you so much trouble...

I...I'm so sorry, Kimie...

♪ Rain, rain, let it storm
'Cause I'm a happy fella
Rain, rain, I'm safe and warm
Under Mom's umbrella ♪

.....

Gen...

What, Mama?

233

Sob... Thank you so much, Gen, for what you did... I'm sorry I made it so difficult for you...

D-don't cry, Mama. You'll make me cry, too...!

Waah! Don't cry, Mama!

Sob...

Sob... Sob...

Waahh!!

The atomic bomb created hell for the dying, and hell for the living. The bitter tears of the survivors fell throughout the land...

About Project Gen

Namie Asazuma
Coordinator, Project Gen

In the pages of *Barefoot Gen*, Keiji Nakazawa brings to life a tragedy unlike any that had ever befallen the human race before. He does not simply depict the destructive horror of nuclear weapons, but tells of the cruel fate they visited upon victims and survivors in the years to come. Yet Gen, the young hero of this story, somehow manages to overcome one hardship after another, always with courage and humor. *Barefoot Gen's* tale of hope and human triumph in the face of nuclear holocaust has inspired volunteer translators around the world, as well as people working in a variety of other media. Over the years *Gen* has been made into a three-part live-action film, a feature-length animation film, an opera, and a musical.

The first effort to translate *Barefoot Gen* from the original Japanese into other languages began in 1976, when Japanese peace activists Masahiro Oshima and Yukio Aki walked across the United States as part of that year's Transcontinental Walk for Peace and Social Justice. Their fellow walkers frequently asked them about the atomic bombing of Hiroshima, and one of them happened to have a copy of *Hadashi no Gen* in his backpack. The Americans on the walk, astonished that an atomic bomb survivor had written about it in cartoon form, urged their Japanese friends to translate it into English. Upon returning to Japan, Oshima and Aki founded Project Gen, a non-profit, all-volunteer group of young Japanese and Americans living in Tokyo, to do just that. Project Gen went on to translate the first four volumes of *Barefoot Gen* into English. One or more of these volumes have also been published in French, German, Italian, Portuguese, Swedish, Norwegian, Indonesian, Tagalog, and Esperanto.

By the 1990s Project Gen was no longer active. In the meantime, author Keiji Nakazawa had gone on to complete ten volumes of *Gen*, and expressed his wish to see the entire story made available to non-Japanese readers. Parts of the first four volumes had also been abridged in translation. A new generation of volunteers responded by reviving Project Gen and producing a new, complete and unabridged translation of the entire Gen series.

The second incarnation of Project Gen got its start in Moscow in 1994, when a Japanese student, Minako Tanabe, launched "Project Gen in Russia" to translate *Gen* into Russian. After publishing the first three volumes in Moscow, the project relocated to Kanazawa, Japan, where volunteers Yulia Tachino and Namie Asazuma had become acquainted with *Gen* while translating a story about Hiroshima into Russian. The Kanazawa volunteers, together with Takako Kanekura in Russia, completed Russian volumes 4 through 10 between 1999 and 2001.

In the spring of 2000, the Kanazawa group formally established a new Project Gen in Japan. Nine volunteers spent the next three years translating all ten volumes of *Gen* into English. The translators are Kazuko Futakuchi, Michael Gordon, Kyoko Honda, Yukari Kimura, Nobutoshi Kohara, Kiyoko Nishita, George Stenson, Michiko Tanaka, and Kazuko Yamada.

In 2002, author Keiji Nakazawa put the Kanazawa team in contact with Alan Gleason, a member of the first Project Gen, who introduced them to Last Gasp of San Francisco, publisher of the original English translation of *Gen*. Last Gasp agreed to publish the new, unabridged translation of all ten volumes, of which this book is one.

In the hope that humanity will never repeat the terrible tragedy of the atomic bombing, the volunteers of Project Gen want children and adults all over the world to hear Gen's story. Through translations like this one, we want to help Gen speak to people in different countries in their own languages. Our prayer is that *Barefoot Gen* will contribute in some small way to the abolition of nuclear weapons before this new century is over.

Write to Project Gen c/o Asazuma, Nagasaka 3-10-20, Kanazawa 921-8112, Japan

Special Acknowledgement
The following people (as well as many who wish to remain anonymous)
contributed generously to our Kickstarter campaign and made these
hardcover editions of *Barefoot Gen* possible.

A. MacBride

A. T. Warren

A. Waller Hastings

Aabra Jaggard

Aaron B Reiser

Aaron Diamond

Aaron J. Schibik

Abhilash Sarhadi

Ada Palmer

Adam Christopher Bryant

Adam Doochin

Adam Meyers

Adrienne Marie Núñez

Agustin Chancusi

Akio Duffy

Alan Zabaro

Alenka Figa

Alex Fitch

Alex Ponomareff

Alex Stevenson

Alexander Hoffman

Alexis A Candelaria

Ali T. Kokmen

Alison Davila

Alok Karande

AM

Amanda Burdic

Amanda, Keagan, and Andromeda O'Mara

Amberly Maxwell

Amy Heaney

Amy Rachels

Amy Watson

Andrea Peitsch

Andrew Lohmann

Andrey Novoseltsev

Andy Holman

Angela Bacchi

Anne-Scott Whitmire

Annie Koyama

Arianne Hartsell-Gundy

Arthur Murakami

Asahiko Matsuda

Ash Brown

Ashley Hernandez

Avelino Morais

Avi Finkel

B. Wilks

Badou Jobe

Barbara Lindsey

Bears Den Mountain Lodge

Ben Laverock

Benjamin Sussman

Benjamin Woo

Bernd the Anon

Beth Campbell

Beth Lonsinger

billy pete

Blue Delliquanti

Bob Culley

bowerbird!

Brad Ander

Brent Van Keulen

Bryan Gaffin

Cabel Sasser

Caitlin Huddleston

Candise Branum

Cara Averna

Carl K.H.

Carlos Bergfeld

Cedric Tisserand

Chikada, Hibiki (fireworks.vc)

Chris Lepkowski

Chris Patti

Chris Shepard

Christian Kaw

Christopher Charles Reed

Clay Nash

Cody Billings

Corey Proft

Cynthia Oshiro

dajomu

Dan and Ellen Wasil

Daniel Cahill

Daniel Oliveira Carn

Daniel Schneider

Daniella Orihuela-Gruber

Danielle Keenan

Dave Johnston

David & Sinda Eggerman

David Lee

David Toccafondi

Denise Larson

Dennis Smith

Derick Peterson

Deter Clawmute

Don Van Horn

Donald Scott

Donna Almendrala

Dorian Bell

Doug Redway

Doug Wilder

Douglas Candano

D-Rock

Dus T'

Dylan Cheung

Dylan Fields

Eileen Kaur Alden

Elaine Loftus Loeb

Eleanor Walker

Elisha Rush

Ellen Jane Keenan

Ellen Power

Ellen Yu

Elliott Walker

Emily Hui

Emily Lakin

Emmanuel D'Hoop

Eric Agena

Eric Kim

Eric Phipps

Erick Reilly

Erika Ray

Evan Ritchie

Eve Turner-Lee

Eyeball Kicks

Fred Burke

G.M. Harvey

Gabe Lowendick

Gabriel Bravo Gallardo

Gary D. Simmons

Gary Tanigawa

Genta Mochizawa

George Peter Dimos

Gina Curtice

Graham Kolbeins

Gregory Prout

Guy Thomas

H.Dannoue

Hans Eric Svensson

Harris Fish

Hart Larrabee

Heather Skweres

Heidi von Markham

Helen Koyama

Hikky Yoshida

Hillary Harris Moldovan

Holly Tomren

Hollyann Wood

Ian Harker

Isabel Samaras

Ismael F. Salazar Jr.

Ivory Madison & Abraham Mertens

J. Christina Smith

J. Driscoll

J. Torres

J.R. Pas

Jackie Fox

Jackie Z.

Jacob Ryan Larson

Jake Pushinsky

James A. Hardi

James Prevott

James R. Bradshaw

James Turnbull

James Wight

Jane Mahoney

Jared Brock

Jared Konopitski

Jason beirens

Jason Tuason

Jay Perry

JB Segal

Jeff Newelt

Jeffrey Kahn

Jeffrey Meyer

Jen Crothers

Jen Propst

<3 Jeska Kittenbrink

Jill DeLong

Jim DelRosso

Jim Kosmicki

Jingran Wang

Jocelyne Allen

John "Boother" Booth

John Kyritsis

John Madigan IV

Johnny Mayall

Jon Kelly

Jon Parrish

Jonathan Shaver

José Loureiro

Joseph Kurachi Luk

Joseph P. Young

Joshua Drescher

Joshua Dunh

Julian Khaw

Julie Reiser

Julitta R. McIntire-Federico

Junko Mizuno

Justin Harman

Karin Wilson

Karl Brian Arcadio

Kat Kan

Katy Costello

Kayoko.A

Kazue Evans

Kelly Winquist

Kelsey C

Kendell Briggs

Kent K. Barnes

Kevin J. Maroney

Kevin Robinson

Kimberly A. Gordon

Kimiaki Suzuki

Kohji 'osa' Osamura

Kory Cerjak

Kristina Elyse Butke

Kristine Anstine

Kumar Sivasubramanian

Kurtis Ray Foster

Kwame N. Akosah

Leanna Lucas

Leen Isabel

legalmoon

Linda Stevens

Linda Yau

Lisa Martincik

Liz Davis

Loren Rhoads

Luan Resende

Lucas Aubrey Paynter

Luke White

Lynne Wooddell and Family

M

M. Griffiths

M.R. Innes

Maggie Young

Mahlon Landis

Maiji/Mary Huang

Marc Escanuelas

Marc Lee

Marc St-Jacques

Marcel Wienen

margaret miller

Mariell Leniuk

Marisa McFarlane

Mark Hartsuyker

Marla Greenwald and Erin Sparling

Mary C. Carroll

Masahiro Kitagawa

Masako I.

Matt Adrian

Matt Parrillo

Matteo Gilebbi

Matthew and Crystalyn Hodgkins

Matthew Mizenko

McCausland

Meagan Lowell Phillips

Mel Smith

Melanie Gillman

Michael Arroyo

Michael C. Stewart

Michael Czobit

Michael John Constantine

Michael MacBride

Michael Pang

Michael Rock

Michael Tannenbaum

Michael Thaler and Inna Guzenfeld

Michelle C.

Michelle Stoliker

Michiko Byers

Mike Borch

Mike Davis

Mike Dawson

Mission: Comics & Art

Monique G.

Naadir Jeewa

Nancy Chan

Nancy Ruan

Nathan Schreiber

Nathan Young

Nathaniel Merchant

Niall John James MacDougall

Nicole Compliment

Nicole Fabricand-Person

Nina Matsumoto

Odette Christensen

Odyssey Publications

Olivia Eirene Luna

Olivia Rohan

Olivia Tai

Omar Pineda

Óscar Morales Vivó

OYAJIHAHA

Pascal Hamon

Patricia Wakida

Patrick King

Patrick Leahy

Patrick Montero

Pattie Piotrowski

Paul Freelend

Paul J Hodgeson

Pete Goldie

Peter Munford

Petey Rave

Phaedra Risher

Philip Kinchington

Priya Ananthasankar

Pual N

R Evans

R. Sikoryak

R. Todd Crockett

R~

Rachel "Nausicaa" Tougas

Raina Telgemeier

Rebecca Boldes

Renzo Adler

Richard J. Neil III

Richard Wesley Hooper

Rob Reger

Robert Altomare

Robert Duncan

Robert Paul Weston

Robert Rosendahl

Rochelle Claire Brown

Rodrigo Ortiz Vinholo

Ronald Stewart

Rosanne Nagy

Royce Engemann

Russell Martens

Ruth Ilano

Ryan Lynch

Ryan Sands

Sadie McFarlane

Samuel Henley

Sarah Rich

Sawa Hotta

Scott Rubin

Sean C Kershaw

Sean Kleefeld

Seiko Yoshina

Sergio Goncalves Proenca

Sergio Segovia Cervantes

Sharon Leong

Shaun Huseman

Shelby McGowan

Shervyn

Shiro H.

Siddharth Gupta

Soko Yamamoto

Sonia Harris

Sophie Muller

Stacey Ransom & Jason Mitchell

Stephen Schloss

Steve & Ana Hart

Steve Laflef

Steve Leialoha and Trina Robbins

Steven Darrall

Steven M. Jankowski

Susanna Hough

Sutter Kane Haggblom

T.M. Finney

Tabi Joy

Takahiro and Molly Kitamura

Tatsuo Senshu Ph.D

Terry W. McCammon II

Tetsuya Ishibashi

The Beguiling Books & Art

The Chou Malpicas

The Hoffman Family

The Kostelecky Family

The Land of Obscusion

theRat

Thomas Lloyd

Thomas Pand

Thorsten Gruber

Timothy Rottenberg

Tomislav Jelenkovic

Tony Bennett

Torsten Adair

TOUYAMA Jun-ichi

Treve Hodsman

Tshihide Satoh

Tsuyoshi Ogawa

Tyler Bibbey

Varun Gupta

Vivian Kokot

W.Schiller

Wesley Holtkamp

Wilma Jandoc Win

Yellow T

Zac Clarke

Zach Powers

Zach Van Stanley

Zach Von Joo

Zachary Clemente

Zack Davisson

琴線計画

近田火日輝

"I named my main character Gen in the hope that he would become a root or source of strength for a new generation of mankind—one that can tread the charred soil of Hiroshima barefoot, feel the earth beneath its feet, and have the strength to say "no" to nuclear weapons... I myself would like to live with Gen's strength—that is my ideal, and I will continue pursuing it through my work."

— Keiji Nakazawa (1939-2012)

Keiji Nakazawa retired from cartooning in 2009. He continued to lecture throughout Japan about the experience of atomic bomb victims, until his death in Hiroshima in 2012, at age 73. He is survived by his wife, daughter, and grandchildren.